VOLUME 4   **2024**

HAYMANOT JOURNAL

SGH MAMHERS (board): Vincent Bacote,
Vince L. Bantu, Quonekuia Day, Carolyn Palmer,
Cleotha Robertson, Nicholas Rowe, Lori Banfield, Jaclyn Williams

GENERAL KATABI
VINCE L. BANTU

Meachum School of Haymanot

Copyright © 2024 by Vince L. Bantu, Editor
www.meachum.org

All rights reserved.
No part of this book may be reproduced or transmitted in any form or by any means, electronic or mechanical, including photocopying, recording, video, or by any information or retrieval system, without prior written permission from the publisher except for the use of brief quotations in a book review.

Published in the United States by Meachum School of Haymanot
PO Box 142799
Saint Louis, Missouri 63114
www.meachum.org

ISBN: 978-1-7357495-8-7 (paperback)
ISBN: 978-1-7357495-3-2 (ebook)

All scripture quotations, unless otherwise indicated, are taken from the NASB, NRSV, NIV, Lexham English Bible (LEB), and Nestle-Aland Greek New Testament (Novum Testamentum Graece) 28th Edition.

Printed in the United States of America

Table of Contents

1. Introduction 1
   Vince L. Bantu

   Sankofa
   Umfundi: Nicholas Rowe

2. "Jesus and the Disinherited: The Enduring
   Presence of Christians of the Maghreb During the
   Earliest Centuries of Islamic Rule". 3
   Vince L. Bantu

3. "A Reading of the American Evangelical Tradition
   Through the Paradigm of African American Religion:
   Afro-Evangelicalism in the Antebellum World" 18
   Jessica N. Janvier

   Haymanot
   Umfundi: Vincent Bacote

4. "Horus and Jesus: Similarities, Differences,
   and Their Implications" 34
   Erika Brown

5. "Reimagining the Historically Black Church's Missional
   Ecclesiology: Serving the Ger in Our Midst" 47
   Corey Lee

   Ujamaa
   Umfundi: Lori Banfield

6. "Embodied Remembrance: Attachment-Narrative
   Reflections on the Spiritually Resilient Voice
   of the Martyrs" 63
   Lori E. Banfield

7. "Progressing Together: A Gospelist Approach on
   Addressing Racial Discrimination within the Workplace". . . . 74
   Charonda Woods-Boone

Book Reviews

"Review of Kelly Brown Douglas's *Resurrection Hope: A Future Where Black Lives Matter*" 90
Leon Harris

"Review of Lisa M. Bowens and Dennis R. Edwards's *Do Black Lives Matter? How Christian Scriptures Speak to Black Empowerment*" 95
Kenneth Reid

"Review of Andrea Myers Achi's *Africa and Byzantium*" 100
Charonda Woods-Boone

Introduction

Welcome to the Fourth Volume of the *Haymanot Journal*

The *Haymanot Journal* publishes the proceedings of the Annual Meeting of the Society of Gospel Haymanot (SGH). SGH is a consortium of Black scholars of biblical, theological, and religious studies that are dedicated to the proclamation of the Bisrat (Gospel) of Jesus Christ, the authority of the Word of Tilli (Old Nubian "God"), the liberation of the marginalized, and the embracing of African-descended cultural identity. The theological landscape of academic institutions is characterized, for the most part, by a liberal-conservative binary, of which the majority of Black scholars follow the former trend. Meanwhile, the rich tradition of the historical Black Church—one that holds equally to the universal truth of the Bisrat and God's call upon His people for the liberation of the marginalized—is largely absent from graduate institutions of theological education. As daughters and sons of the Black Church and scholars of religious studies, the SGH exists to: 1.) bring the theological perspective of the dominant Black Church—which we call Gospel Haymanot—into conversation with mainstream academia; 2.) to create a scholarly community for Gospelist scholars; 3.) to reclaim a Black theology that is grounded in the authority of the Word of God; and, 4.) to produce Gospelist scholarship that serves the Global Church and institutions of theological education.

The *Haymanot Journal* exists to serve these goals. If one were to search for academic monographs and journal articles on Black

Theology or written by Black theologians, they would overwhelmingly represent a theological perspective foreign to the majority of the Black Church. The *Haymanot Journal* exists to provide peer-reviewed scholarship from Black scholars that hold to the Bisrat and to Black liberation. This volume is organized into four disciplines framed by our African forms of knowledge and being: *Dersat* (a Geʽez—classical Ethiopic—term meaning "biblical exegesis"); *Sankofa* (an Akan concept meaning "go back and get it" in the sense of knowing and reclaiming one's history); *Haymanot* (a Geʽez—classical Ethiopic—term meaning "doctrine," "faith," or "theology"); and *Ujamaa* (a Swahili term meaning "collective responsibility" or "family," in the sense of practical ministry and community development). Each paper has been edited by Umfundi (Xhosa terms for "reader") who are discipline specialists as well as the general Katabi (Geʽez—classical Ethiopic—term for "scribe" or "editor"). Each article was presented at the fourth Annual Meeting of the SGH which was held in the fall of 2023. I pray that the scholarship contained in this volume will enrich the academy, support the Church and glorify the Lord Jesus Christ.

By the grace of Tilli,

Vince L. Bantu

Jesus and the Disinherited: The Enduring Presence of Christians of the Maghreb During the Earliest Centuries of Islamic Rule

Vince L. Bantu

"The Muslim invasion of North Africa wiped out the Christian presence here." Habib Bourguiba, the first president of the Republic of Tunisia, said this in an interview in 1962.¹ It is commonly assumed that the Islamic Conquest of the Maghreb in the late seventh century eradicated North African Christianity.² However, an increasing amount of scholarship over the last few decades has provided nuance to this dominant narrative. While detailed reports on the nature of North African Christianity are lacking, evidence indicates a North African Church that continued to operate well into the dotowan period.³ Much of the information on North African Christianity under Islamic rule indicates a continued relationship between the Roman Church and Christians of the Maghreb. However, there are indications

---

¹ Andrew Borowiec, *Modern Tunisia: A Democratic Apprenticeship* (Westport, CT: Praeger, 1998), 13.
² C. J. Speel, "The Disappearance of Christianity from North Africa in the Wake of the Rise of Islam," *Church History* 29, no. 4 (1960): 379–397.
³ An Africanist equivalent to "medieval period," referring to the united Nubian kingdom of Dotawo.

of another patriarchal connection with other African Christians living under Islamic rule. This paper will explore the evidence for the persistence of Christianity in the Maghreb under Islamic dominance and the ability of this evidence to understand the theological landscape of dotowan North African Christianity.

One of the earliest examples of North African Christianity following the Islamic Conquest is also one of the only surviving Christian texts from this region: the *Concordia Canonum* of Cresconius the African. The text provides a date of 570 CE; however, most scholars date the text to the late seventh century.[4] The *Concordia Canonum* is a lengthy compilation of liturgical, ecclesiastical, and ascetic regulations taken from various church councils. While the text does not provide significant information on the nature of the North African Church, it is worth noting that Cresconius draws heavily upon the canons of the Council of Chalcedon (451 CE). This would indicate that North African Christians were still heavily Chalcedonian, the same as their predecessors. This is of note, given that the Christian communities that continued to thrive on the African continent in the following centuries adopted a Miaphysite Christology. Other canons in the *Concordia Canonum* include regulations for readmitting lapsed Christians into the community of catechumens.[5] These textual features indicate that Cresconius represented a continuing Christian tradition that continued with the dominant church of prior times, a tradition that differed from the Miaphysite and Donatist communities. It is perhaps not surprising that this significant representation of North African Christianity emerged at a time after the defeat of the Romans at the hands of the Rashidun Caliphate, but likely before the fall of Carthage in 698 CE. It may have been the case that the North African Church was still operating much as usual in the late seventh century.

---

[4] David E. Wilhite, *Ancient African Christianity: An Introduction to a Unique Context and Tradition* (New York: Routledge, 2017), 330.
[5] Cresconius the African, *Canonum Concordia* (Migne, *PL* **88**.874).

Indeed, Pope Gregory II expressed concern about Donatist communities persisting in North Africa. Gregory ordained Boniface as bishop over Germania in response to increasing demand for ecclesiastical support in this region. Gregory wrote a letter in 722 CE after Boniface's ordination, in which the Pope cautioned the newly ordained bishop against illegitimate ordinations. Gregory identified people with disabilities, men who had remarried, people with other civic responsibilities, illiterate people, or anyone with "any inferior condition." Gregory placed his most significant attention on Africans, whom he also forbade Boniface to ordain: "That for no reason he [Boniface] should not accept Africans, people who feign ecclesiastical orders here and there, because it has been demonstrated often that among them some are Manicheans, others rebaptized. One should not endeavor to diminish the ministries and the adornment of the church and whatever properties there are, but to increase them."[6] Not surprisingly, Donatist communities would continue in the earliest decades of Islamic dominance in North Africa. However, Gregory's totalizing rhetoric is significant. The Pope not only cautioned against receiving Donatists or "rebaptized" for ordination but also levied the prohibition against all "Africans." Such language indicates that the Pope perceived Christians throughout Africa as Donatists. Such an idea evokes the well-known debate in scholarship regarding the claim that Donatism was a more indigenously African expression of Christianity than the Catholic Church.[7] While this debate is beyond the scope of this study, Gregory's letter does not represent a decidedly supportive perspective of the African Church from the perspective of Europe. If such

---

[6] Gregory II, "Lettre du pape Grégoire II à un peuple germanique," in *Le dossier du donatisme, t. 1: Des origins à la mort de Constance II (303–361)*, ed. Jean-Louis Maier (Berlin: Akademie-Verlag, 1987), 395. All translations of non-English texts were done by the author.
[7] Frend proposed this view in W.H.C. Frend, *The Donatist Church: A Movement of Protest in Roman North Africa*, 2nd ed. (New York: Oxford University Press, 2003), 336. For a response to Frend's theory, see Maureen A. Tilley, *The Donatist World* (Minneapolis, MN: Fortress Press, 1997), 8.

an attitude towards the African Church persisted among other European ecclesiastical leaders, the decline of North African Christianity would not be surprising.

By the ninth century, writers such as Florus of Lyon lamented what he perceived as the disappearance of Christianity in North Africa. Florus specifically wrote about the disappearance of the relics of Cyprian. The ninth-century Arab-Egyptian historian Ibn ʿAbd al-Hakam provided an account of the Arab conquest of the Maghreb, indicating that Christians continued to inhabit the region as religious minorities. After defeating the Imazighen queen Kahina,[8] the Umayyad Arab general Hassan ibn al-Nuʿman imposed the poll tax upon the Christian population of Africa: "Hassan departed, and he settled in the region of Kairouan, Africa of today. And he built a central mosque, he administered its administrations, and he imposed the tax on the non-Arabs of Africa and those who, along with them, profess Christianity—the Amazigh [ربربل], mostly from the Baranis and a few from the Butrs. Hassan remained at his post until the country was established."[9] The report of Ibn Abd al-Hakam indicates that the Christian population of North Africa would have persisted as subjugated minorities. This report further indicates that the presence of "foreigners"—likely Roman citizens from across the Mediterranean—also continued to live as Christians in North Africa into Islamic times.

Indeed, a ninth-century Spanish martyr, Eulogius of Córdoba, attested to the presence of a persecuted Christian community in North Africa. The Umayyad-controlled Emirate of Córdoba, under the direction of Caliphs Abd ar-Rahman II (822–852 CE) and Muhammad I of Córdoba (852–886 CE), executed some fifty Córdoban

---

[8] The accepted name for indigenous North Africans, often erroneously referred to by the colonial name "Berbers."
[9] Ibn Abd al-Hakam, *Futuh Ifrqiya wa-l-Andalus*, ed. Albert Gateau (Algiers: Editions Carbonel, 1942), 74–76.

Christians, many of whom had converted from Islam.[10] One of these martyrs—George—was sent by the abbot of the Mar Saba Monastery in Jerusalem to collect alms from the Christians in North Africa. Because of the persecution of Christians in Africa and Spain, George desired to go "to the Kingdom of the Christians, that is, France."[11] While Eulogius did not have first-hand knowledge of Christians in North Africa, the relaying of George's interaction with North African Christians is plausible. Indeed, suppose Eulogius's account can be accepted. In that case, it is noteworthy that the abbot of Mar Saba would consider the North African monastic communities as a source of financial support for Christians in other regions.

The tenth-century North African historian Ibn al-Saghir attested to the presence of Christians during his lifetime in the Rustamid capital city of Tahert (modern Tiaret, Algeria). When local imams fought for control of Tahert, the Christians allied themselves with Abu Bakr, who sought control of the Rustamid dynasty: "And this coalition reached Abu Bakr and his associates quickly gathered around him, those of the Christians [المسيحيين], the Rustamids and others. And the people marched from the top of the city from the eastern direction. And the relatives, followers and associates of Abu Bakr marched from the west."[12] Abu Bakr's rival, Abu Yaqzan, was victorious and exercised significant control of religious dynamics for the Muslim community.[13] The eleventh-century Spanish cartographer al-Bakri mentioned the existence of a Christian church and shrines in the city of Tlemcen

---

[10] Mikla Levy-Rubin and Benjamin Z. Kedar, "A Spanish Source on Mid-Ninth-Century Mar Saba and a Neglected Sabaite Martyr," in *The Sabaite Heritage in the Orthodox Church from the Fifth Century to the Present*, ed. Joseph Patrich (Leuven: Peeters, 2001), 63.

[11] Eulogius, *Memorialis Sanctorum*, 788.

[12] Ibn al-Saghir, *Akkbār al-a'imma l-Rustumiyyīn*, ed. A.C. Motylinski (Paris: Ernest Leroux, 1907), 36. See also Virginie Prevost, "The Last Native Christian Communities of North Africa," in *Revue de l'histoire des religions* 224, no. 4 (2007): 465, https://doi.org/10.4000/rhr.5401.

[13] Ibn al-Saghir, *Akkbār al-a'imma l-Rustumiyyīn*, 46–47.

in modern Algeria.[14] The fact that al-Bakri only mentions a Christian remnant and a functioning church indicates the possibility that Tlemcen may have had a Christian majority during the eleventh century.

The twelfth-century Spanish historian al-Idrisi describes the Tunisian oasis town of Gapsa (Capsa) as a central city whose inhabitants continued to speak Latin during his lifetime:

> Capsa is a beautiful city with a wall. There is a flowing river whose water is better than the water of Castilia. In its center is a spring whose name is Al-Tarmidz. In it are markets that are stocked and do a lot of business. The factories located there are competent . . . its people have become Berberized [متبربرون] and most of them speak African-Latin [الطينى الافريقى].[15]

The presence of Latin-speaking North Africans in southern Tunisia during the twelfth century indicates the persistence of Christianity during this time. While al-Idrisi does not comment on the religious affiliation of the inhabitants of Gapsa, the mention of Latin speakers would indicate an affiliation with Christianity.[16] Prevost points out that "African-Latin" refers to both the Latin language and Romance dialects such as Spanish or Italian. Therefore, al-Idrisi, a Spanish and Latin speaker, identified the language of Gapsa as a native Amazigh Latin dialect.[17] The survival of Latin into Almohad times can serve

---

[14] Tarek Ladjal, "The Christian Presence in North Africa under Almoravids Rule (1040–1147 CE): Coexistence or Eradication?" *Cogent Arts & Humanities* 4, no. 1 (2017): 9.

[15] Al-Idrisi, *Description de l'Afrique et de l'Espagne*, ed. R. Dozy and M. J. De Goeje (Leiden: Brill, 1866), 104–5.

[16] A similar conclusion is found in Mohamed Talbi, "Le Christianisme maghrébin: de la conquête musulmane à sa disparition," in *Conversion and Continuity: Indigenous Christian Communities in Islamic Lands: Eighth to Eighteenth Centuries*, ed. Michael Gervers and Ramzi Jibran Bikhazi (Toronto, ON: Pontifical Institute of Mediaeval Studies, 1990), 339. Talbi understands the dialect to which Al-Idiris refers as a local, Amazigh dialect of Latin. See also Peter C. Scales, *The Fall of the Caliphate of Córdoba: Berbers and Andalusis in Conflict* (Leiden: Brill, 1994), 147.

[17] Prevost, "Last Native Christian Communities," 479.

as an indication of the survival of Christianity. Latin was extensively associated with Christianity in North Africa, while Punic and Amazigh (Ancient Lybic) were not used in biblical translation or liturgy. For this reason, the most common reason scholars have given for the disappearance of Christianity in North Africa was the exodus of Roman elites.[18] With the departures of Latin-speaking elites, Christians would not have had access to bishops who could perform the rites of baptism and Eucharist. Latin speakers' survival in Gapsa calls into question the familiar narrative of Latin and Christianity disappearing after the Islamic Conquest.

Archaeological evidence further indicates the persistence of Christianity in the Islamic Maghreb. The central-western Tunisian city of Sbeitla had several churches that do not seem to have been destroyed or repurposed after the Conquest.[19] Indeed, some of these churches still seem to have been in use during the tenth century. There were even examples of new churches being built during Islamic rule. An individual named Qustas requested that a church be built in the capital city of Kairouan. Furthermore, Christian funerary inscriptions attest to the presence of Christians and church officials in the tenth century.[20] The fourteenth-century Tunisian historian Ibn Khaldun reported that there were Christians in the Libyan town of Nefzaoua: "In it are found some Franks living under the tax and residing with protection since the treaty of the [Islamic] Conquest, along with their ancestors, until this Conquest."[21] Ibn Khaldun adds that there were "Frankish"

---

[18] Talbi, "Christianisme maghrébin," 344.
[19] Noel Duval, *Sbeitla et les églises africaines à deux absides*, vols. 1 & 2 (Paris: 1971, 1973).
[20] Corisande Fenwick, "The Arab Conquests and the End of Ancient Africa?" in *A Companion to North Africa in Antiquity*, ed. R. Bruce Hitchner (Hoboken, NJ: John Wiley & Sons, 2022), 434; see also, Talbi "Christianisme maghrébin," 318; Corisande Fenwick, "Ifriqiya and the Central Maghreb," in *The Oxford Handbook of Islamic Archaeology*, ed. Bethany J. Walker, Timothy Insoll, and Corisande Fenwick (Oxford: Oxford University Press, 2020), 260.
[21] Ibn Khaldun, *Histoire des Berbères et des dynasties musulmanes de l'Afrique Septentrionale*, ed. William M. de Slane, t. 1 (Algiers: Imprimerie du Gourvernement, 1847), 147.

people from Sardinia in Nefzaoua.²² While evidence corroborating the report of Ibn Khaldun is lacking, there is also no plausible reason to doubt the existence of a Frankish-descended Christian community in his native Tunisia during the fourteenth century.

In 1053, the Roman Pope Leo IX wrote a letter to a certain Thomas of Carthage, whom the Pope recognized as the "primate of all of Africa." The purpose of the letter is to clarify that an unnamed North African bishop is not authorized to consecrate bishops or convene local councils with the consent of Thomas, "but the Romans alone were to be pontiffs and to depose bishops and to appoint general councils."²³ Leo recalls the greatness of the Carthaginian bishopric and contrasts the current status of the North African Church, which has "barely five bishops in all of Africa." Multiple times in his letter, Leo refers to two other North African bishops, Peter and John. Unlike the unnamed "Gummian" bishop, Peter and John are legitimate bishops. They are from unspecified regions of North Africa and are required to recognize the primacy of Carthage over North Africa. If Leo's figure of five bishops in North Africa is not an exaggeration, then his letter identifies almost all of the remaining bishops in North Africa during the eleventh century.²⁴ Leo laments the "lack of religion [*defectu religionis*]" in Africa yet commends Thomas, who "awaits the opinion of your mother, the holy Roman Church, from which you took the beginning of the whole Christian religion [*totius Christianæ religionis*]." Leo claims that, as the bishop of Carthage, Thomas is the "first archbishop and greatest metropolitan of all Africa," second only to the authority of the Roman pontiff. The rival bishop remained

---

²² Ibn Khaldun, *Histoire des berbères et des dynasties musulmanes de l'Afrique Septentrionale*, ed. William M. de Slane, t. 3 (Algiers: Imprimerie du Gourvernement, 1856), 156–7.
²³ Leo IX, "Letter to Thomas of Carthage" (Migne, *PL* 143.727–8). See also John Howe, *Before the Gregorian Reform: The Latin Church at the Turn of the First Millennium* (Ithaca, NY: Cornell University Press, 2016), 310.
²⁴ Jonathan Conant, *Staying Roman: Conquest and Identity in Africa and the Mediterranean, 439–700* (Cambridge: Cambridge University Press, 2012), 368.

unnamed and resided in the Gummi region of modern Tunisia. This "Gummian bishop," according to Leo, has no authority to consecrate or depose bishops nor to convene councils without the consent of the Carthaginian bishop. Indeed, Leo contrasts the "Carthaginian Church" with the "Gummian Church," arguing for the latter to be subservient to the former. Leo clarifies that the same hierarchy must persist between Carthage and the Roman pontiff. While Jesus claimed that ecclesial decisions would be bound in heaven, Christ also told Peter that he would be the rock of the Church.[25] For this reason, Thomas has the ability to "examine certain bishops, yet it is not permissible to give a definitive opinion without consulting the Roman Pontiff."[26] Leo ends his short epistle with a charge to Timothy to guard the Catholic Church's interests and uphold Trinitarian doctrine.

Pope Gregory VII (1073–1085 CE) was an essential witness to the presence of Christianity in North Africa in several of his papal letters. Gregory's papacy occurred during the ascendancy of the Almoravid Dynasty (c. 1050–1147 CE), but before this caliphate annexed Al-Andalus (1094 CE). The timeline is significant, given that scholars generally view the deportation of Christians to the Maghreb from Al-Andalus following the annexation as the principal source of dotowan North African Christianity.[27] Before the mass deportation of Spanish Christians to the Maghreb, Gregory engaged significantly with the diminished but active Christian community in North Africa. According to Gregory, the North African church was sparse, but led by a bishop named Cyriacus: "Bishop Gregory, servant of God's servants, to my beloved brother Cyriacus, archbishop of Carthage in Christ, greetings and apostolic blessing. It has arrived to our ears that Africa, which is said to be a part of the world, and which even in ancient times, when Christianity prevailed [*vigente*] there—governed by the

---

[25] Matt. 16:18; 18:18–20.
[26] Leo IX, "Letter to Thomas of Carthage," 728.
[27] Ladjal, "The Christian Presence in North Africa," 3.

greatest number of bishops—has come to such a danger that it does not have three bishops to ordain a[nother] bishop."[28] Gregory also indicates that there was another leader at Cyriacus—perhaps another bishop—who was recently ordained by Rome. The letter recommends that Cyriacus and his unnamed colleague choose someone to be sent to Rome, that they might be ordained bishop. The letter expressed "sympathy for the few laborers in the greatest field [*in maximo agro paucis operariis*]." Receiving a qualified bishop for North Africa would lighten the load of Cyriacus and cause the "Christian people [*Christiana gens*] to rejoice."

Gregory VII wrote another letter to "the clergy and people of Hippo in Mauritania Sitifensis, that is, in Africa,"[29] in order to confirm the consecration of a bishop sent to Rome. This letter attests to the presence of Christians in regions outside of Carthage, which is the city mentioned in most dotowan sources indicating Christians. In the same letter, Gregory exhorts the Mauritanian clergy to accept the bishop so that "the Muslims [*Sarracenorum*] who are around you, seeing the sincerity of your faith, also the purity of mutuality between you of divine charity and brotherly love will be provoked by your deeds rather than to rivalry, which [leads] to contempt of the Christian faith." The question of Christian-Muslim relations in the Maghreb occupied the attention of another epistle of Gregory VII, in which he exhorted the believers of Carthage "to lay aside their enmities, and bear with patience the attacks of the Saracens."[30] He wrote his letter to address the question of an attack by certain Christians upon the aforementioned bishop Cyriacus. Gregory appeals to the sacrifice of Jesus Christ and the persecution of the Apostles, exhorting the Carthaginian church to bear "the arms of the Saracens" with the same spiritual resolve. The believers are to rejoice in suffering, avoid quarreling,

---

[28] Gregory VII, "Letter 19," in *Opera pars prima* (Migne, *PL* 148.449).
[29] Gregory VII, "Letter 20," in *Opera pars prima* (Migne, *PL* 148.450).
[30] Gregory VII, "Letter 22," in *Opera pars prima* (Migne, *PL* 148.305).

and be subject to governmental authorities.³¹ Gregory's citation of Romans 13 brings together his concerns about enduring Islamic persecution and avoiding divisions within the church: "When, then, the apostle preached obedience to the worldly powers, how much more to the spiritual ones, and to those who have the place of Christ among Christians?" Gregory then addresses the chief question of the beating of Bishop Cyriacus:

> This, dear children, I ponder with sighing, I write with tears, and I send to you with deep pain in my heart. Indeed, it has come to our ears, that some of you [are] unreligious [*irreligiose*] in the law of Christ, [and] against Christ, our venerable brother Cyriacus, your archbishop and teacher. And more so, indeed, you have so accused your Christ before the Saracens, and have so torn him up with quarrels, that he was numbered among robbers, and truly was beaten naked.³²

Gregory threatens the Carthaginian Christians with anathematization and exhorts them to repent of their assault upon Cyriacus. In yet another letter addressed to Cyriacus, Gregory "praises his [Cyriacus'] consistence, because he patiently bore the insults of the Saracens and bad Christians [*malorum Christianorum*], and refused to have ordinances in the presence of King Henry. He is encouraged to persevere. God is beseeched for the African church."³³ Cyriacus continues to deal with "a double struggle" both of Islamic persecution and Christian schisms due to "pseudo-daughters of the Church." The incipit of Letter 23 indicates that Gregory is addressing the investiture controversy and specifically critiques King Henry IV: "But thank God! For in the midst of a nation of perverse and perverted faith [*nationis pravæ et perversæ fidei*] your consistence, like a light, became so well known to all, that

---

³¹ Rom. 13:1–7.
³² Gregory VII, "Letter 22," 306.
³³ Gregory VII, "Letter 23," in *Opera pars prima* (Migne, *PL* 148.307).

when you were presented before a royal audience, you would rather be condemned by various tortures than to be celebrated by a king commanding contrary to the ordinations of the holy canons." Gregory encouraged Cyriacus to remain steadfast in the orthodox faith, even to the point of martyrdom. The Pope cried out to God: "Therefore, although we are absent in body, yet present in spirit, we insist on mutual consolation of letters, as often as opportunity allows, and constantly beseech Almighty God that he himself may at last deem the African Church [*Ecclesiam Africanum*] worthy to look upon, which has been suffering for a long time, and shaken by waves of various disturbances."[34] Gregory's request for mutual correspondence seems to indicate a lack of communication from the church of Carthage. Yet, Gregory's extensive correspondence with Cyriacus points to an active North African church before the Andalusian deportations. Furthermore, the association of Gregory and Cyriacus indicates that the Carthaginian bishop would have led a Chalcedonian Church in communion with Rome and not Alexandria. The lack of internal evidence from North African Christians during the eleventh century renders any suggestions as to the theological landscape of dotowan North African Christianity tentative. Nevertheless, Gregory's mention of divisive factions in the North African church indicates a variety of ecclesial camps. Indeed, Egyptian Christian sources from Fatimid times indicate the presence of Miaphysite Christianity in the Maghreb.

The tenth-century Egyptian historian Severus ibn al-Muqaffa compiled a massive work of Egyptian Christian history, referred to as the *Arabic History of the Patriarchs of Alexandria (AHPA)*. This work narrates the history of the Egyptian Church through the perspective and biographies of its patriarchs, or Apa ("father"). Severus drew upon earlier sources in Greek and Coptic, which were translated and united with contemporary Arabic material. In the biography of

---

[34] Gregory VII, "Letter 23," 308.

Patriarch Joseph I of Alexandria (831–849 CE), the *AHPA* identifies the jurisdiction of the See of Mark thusly:

> And because of the abundance with which this good shepherd [Patriarch Abba Joseph] cared for his flock and sacrificed himself for his lambs, he ordained many bishops and dispatched them to every location [*mawḍi'*] under the throne of Lord Mark the evangelist, which include Africa ['āfriyqiyat] and the Five Cities and Kairouan ['āl-qiyruw'ān] and Tripoli and the region of Egypt [*kuwrat miṣr*] and Ethiopia ['āl-ḥabešat] and Nubia ['āl-nuwbat].³⁵

According to the *AHPA*, the Maghreb was part of the Patriarchate of Alexandria. This claim contradicts the perspective of the Latin Christian and Arabic Muslim sources of this time, which indicates a continued communion with Rome on the part of the North African church.

Elsewhere in the *AHPA*, "Berbers" feature as the abductors of Christians in the monasteries Scetis.³⁶ During the patriarchate of Theodore (731–743 CE), the "Berbers of the district of Africa [البربر من اعمال افريقية]" appear in the *AHPA* as neither Christian nor Muslim.³⁷ Because of the oppressive policies of Ubaid Allah, governor of Egypt, he was banished by his own son to the "Berbers," who, in turn, revolted against his attempts at rule in Africa. The *AHPA* recounted a story where an unnamed Chalcedonian governor of Spain

---

³⁵ Sāwīrus ibn al-Muqaffa', *History of the Patriarchs of the Coptic Church of Alexandria*, trans. and ed. Basil Thomas Alfred Evetts, vol. 1., Patrologia Orientalis t. 1, fasc. 2 (Paris: Firmin-Didot, 1904), 512 [this source will henceforth be referred to as *AHPA*]; "Africa" here likely refers to the region known as Africa Proconsularis in Roman times, the former empire of Carthage, whereas Kairouan lies further south. The term 'āl-ḥabešat is used inconsistently to refer to Nubia and Ethiopia. The *AHPA* later refers to a Pool in Cairo that commemorates a battle with the Nubian King Cyriacus which is called the "Pool of the Habesha ('āl-ḥabešan)," 144.
³⁶ *AHPA* III, 82.
³⁷ *AHPA* III, 87.

came into conflict with Patriarch James (819–830 CE). The Spanish governor was removed from his position, and Patriarch James was exonerated.[38] While this account does not mention the Maghreb, it is significant that this story highlights the Miaphysite Patriarch James' victory over the Chalcedonian Spanish governor. This account could form the backdrop of the *AHPA*'s perspective on the Coptic jurisdiction over the Maghreb. Later, Patriarch James came into conflict with the Andalusian ruler of Egypt—Abd al-Aziz al-Jawari—who desired to control the grain output in Egypt.[39] According to the *AHPA*, al-Jawari was killed while traveling to meet the patriarch, demonstrating God's protection of the Copts under Andalusian rule.

In the thirteenth century, Egyptian perspectives on the Church of the Maghreb indicate that this region was in communion with Rome:

> Northwest Africa: The Apostle Philip—translated as "lover of horses"—preached the gospel in West Africa. [There is a shrine] for Saint John [and a shrine] in the name of the pure virgin Lady Mary, built by a traveling merchant in the year 931 of Alexander [618–619 CE]. Romans [الروم] live in the west of the west and much snow, large hail and strong hail fall there. People and many beasts die there. Carthage: The body of the aforementioned Philip is buried in Carthage.[40]

The text does not confirm or deny the earlier *AHPA*'s report of Alexandrian dominance over the Carthaginian and Libyan churches. The "kingdom to the west" of Carthage could reference Mauritania or Al-Andalus. This text also describes the "Berbers" as the cause of the destruction of Egyptian monasteries: "At the edge of the mountains is a city called Mastayah. At the edge of the mountains is Al-Jizah there

---

[38] *AHPA* IV, 449.
[39] *AHPA* IV, 458.
[40] Ṣamūʾīl al-Suryānī, ed., *Tārīkh ʾabū al-makārim ʿan al-kanāʾis wa-l-adyura fī l-qarn '12' bi-l-wajh al-qablī*, vol. 2 (Cairo, 1999), 144.

are fifty monasteries [دير] with a large population of people, which have been destroyed and burnt by the infidels; that is, at the hands of the Amazigh [البربر] of the Maghreb, who do not know the truth, or observe the law, or distinguish between right and wrong."[41] The text goes on to describe this mountain range as extending from the western Nile Delta to the "entire Western seacoast, all the way to the land of Baraghwatah." Given the author's perspective, it is most likely that such monasteries would have been part of the orthodox—or Miaphysite—community. Therefore, from the perspective of this text, along with the *AHPA*, North Africa maintained a strong Miaphysite Christian community.

Given that most of the sources regarding dotowan North African Christianity come from outside the church of the Maghreb, any conclusions about the nature of this community must be tentative. Recent scholarship has provided a helpful correction to the traditional narrative that North African Christianity died out after the Arab Muslim Conquest. While much of the evidence points to a continuing Roman Christian tradition in North Africa, Coptic sources from this period raise the possibility of a Miaphysite Christian contingent continuing to persist alongside the Roman Chalcedonian community. The absence of Roman imperial authority in the Maghreb, coupled with the Miaphysite dominance of the Egyptian Christian community, may have contributed to the emergence of an anti-Chalcedonian North African church during the dotowan period.

---

[41] Ṣamū'īl al-Suryānī., *Tārīkh 'ābū al-makārim*, 83.

A Reading of the American Evangelical Tradition Through the Paradigm of African American Religion: Afro-Evangelicalism in the Antebellum World[42]

Jessica N. Janvier

"In those days there were thousands of our people who preferred an illiterate man of their own race, who was known to be true to the Evangelical faith, [than] to a white man."[43]

Former slave turned missionary, Thomas Johnson

Prolegomena

"Black Evangelical" is odd and somewhat suspicious terminology today. However, this is not the case for scholars engaged in the study of early African American religion and culture, nor for modern

---

[42] This is essay is based in part on my dissertation submitted to the faculty of Columbia International University. See Jessica Brooks-Janvier, "The Essence of Antebellum Afro-Evangelicalism: A Reading of the Evangelical Tradition Through the Paradigm of African American Religion" (PhD diss., Columbia International University, 2023), https://www.proquest.com/dissertations-theses/essence-antebellum-afro-evangelicalism-reading/docview/3043667086/se-2.

[43] Thomas Johnson, *Twenty-Eight Years A Slave or The Story of My Life in Three Continents* (Bournemouth: W. Mate & Sons, Limited Printers and Publishers, 1909), 64.

ethnographers examining the dominant *orientation* in which African Americans express their Christianity. Within these fields, "Evangelical" is frequently applied descriptively to African American Christianity.

Studies in African American religion depicting the rise of African American Christianity have maintained a connection between early Black Christian identity and theological expression with the antebellum Evangelical movement. This has been the case in the earliest historiography in this discipline. The work of W. E. B. DuBois, *The Negro Church*, initially published in 1903, and Carter G. Woodson's text building on DuBois', *The History of the Negro Church* in 1921, both connect the growth and rise of African American Christianity with Evangelicalism.[44] Albert Raboteau, a preeminent scholar of African and African American religions, maintained the pattern of DuBois and Woodson in connecting the rise of African American Christianity to the rise of Evangelicalism in his influential 1978 work, *Slave Religion* and especially in his subsequent essay "The Black Experience in American Evangelicalism."[45] In both texts, he maintains that Blacks were not passive recipients of White Christianity but formed their own distinctive Evangelical tradition. Following in the steps of his mentor Raboteau, Eddie Glaude sees the development of a distinctive Evangelical tradition among early African American Christians.[46] Marla Fredericks' ethnographic work *Between Sundays*, which focuses on commonplace lay Black Christians, categorized the *kind*

---

[44] W. E. B. DuBois, *The Negro Church* (Eugene, OR: Cascade Books, 2011). See also Carter G. Woodson, *The History of the Negro Church* (Washington, DC: The Associated Publishers, 1921).

[45] Albert J. Raboteau, "The Black Experience in American Evangelicalism: The Meaning of Slavery," in *African-American Religion: Interpretive Essays in History and Culture*, eds. Timothy E. Fulop and Albert J. Raboteau (New York: Routledge, 1997), 90–106.

[46] Eddie Glaude, *Exodus! Religion, Race, and Nation in Early Nineteenth-Century Black America* (Chicago, IL: The University of Chicago Press, 2000), 33.

of Christianity African Americans practiced as "Evangelical."[47] The disassociation between African American Christianity and the Evangelical tradition is one particular to modernity with three main contributing factors.

Factors for Disassociation

First, the contemporary term "Evangelical" in popular American culture has lost the sense of being a reference to a specific *tradition* or *orientation* related to how a particular group of Christians interprets and practices their faith within the larger Christian tradition, which makes them distinct from Roman Catholicism, Eastern and Oriental Orthodoxy, and other forms of Protestantism. George Marsden averred that in terms of beliefs and affirmations, many Black Protestants fit within the Evangelical fold but are not considered "card-carrying evangelical[s]."[48] His basis of determination has to do with self-conscious identification. If "Evangelical" as descriptive nomenclature describes something more than a tradition or orientation, then to what does it refer? For many, this term elicits a socio-political identification. Historian of Evangelicalism Thomas Kidd has noted its association with being "white and Republican."[49] Thus, it is disorienting when scholars of religion, looking at the kind of Christianity most early African American Christians practiced, use the term "Evangelical" to describe their orientation to the faith and the tradition of Christianity.

---

[47] Marla F. Fredericks, *Between Sundays: Black Women and Everyday Struggles of Faith* (Berkeley, CA: University of California Press, 2003), 167. While her study concentrates on Black women, it could easily be applied to Black men in terms of categorizing the tradition of Christianity practiced by both.

[48] George M. Marsden, *Understanding Fundamentalism and Evangelicalism* (Grand Rapids, MI: Eerdmans, 1991), 1–6.

[49] Thomas Kidd, "Polls Show Evangelicals Support Trump. But the Term 'Evangelical' Has Become Meaningless," *Washington Post*, July 22, 2016, https://www.washingtonpost.com/news/acts-of-faith/wp/2016/07/22/polls-show-evangelicals-support-trump-but-the-term-evangelical-has-become-meaningless/.

The term signifies the inverse of their identity to modern, popular ears. However, this points to an underlying historiographical issue.

If "Evangelical" connotes whiteness and Republican politics to modern ears, it is because of the second factor contributing to the modern disassociation between African American Christianity and Evangelicalism, which is historiography. For historians who trace the roots of the tradition that we today refer to as Evangelicalism, the Great Awakening revivals have been a galvanizing point.[50] The Great Awakening revivals were transformative for whites, Blacks, and Native Americans alike in the antebellum period. The revivals produced an atmosphere that allowed African Americans to not only be receivers of the awakenings but also take part in leading them and eventually form their own Christian bodies, many of which are still present today. Nonetheless, American Evangelical historiography has tended to center on white leaders, such as Jonathan Edwards, George Whitefield, and Charles Finney, among many others, while marginalizing their contemporaries, such as Jarena Lee, Lemuel Haynes, and Richard Allen, among many others. While Blacks did not start the Evangelical tradition, they were undoubtedly a part of its building and spread. Allen's spiritual biography is an illustration of this. Describing his vigor and determination to preach and participate in the Evangelical revivals after his conversion, he recounted a time before his settling in Philadelphia, where he led a revival, demonstrating how Blacks were not only participants in early Evangelicalism but were also leaders. He noted,

> We had a glorious meeting. They invited me to stay till Sabbath day and preach for them. I agreed to do so, and preached on Sabbath day to a large congregation of different persuasions,

---

[50] For a short history of how "Evangelical" has been used within Protestantism, see Linford D. Fisher, "Evangelicals and Unevangelicals: The Contested History of a Word, 1500–1950," in *Religion and American Culture: A Journal of Interpretation* 26, no. 2 (2016): 184–226.

and my dear Lord was with me, and I believe there were many souls cut to the heart, and were added to the ministry. They insisted on me to stay longer with them. I stayed and laboured [sic] in Radnor several weeks. Many souls were awakened, and cried aloud to the Lord to have mercy upon them. I was frequently called upon by many inquiring what they should do to be saved. I appointed them to prayer and supplication at the throne of grace, and to make use of all manner of prayer, and pointed them to the invitation of our Lord and Saviour [sic] Jesus Christ, who has said, "Come unto me, all ye that are weary and heavy laden, and I will give you rest." Glory be to God! and now I know he was a God at hand and left not afar off. I preached my farewell sermon, and left these dear people. It was a time of visitation from above. [M]any were the slain of the Lord. Seldom did I ever experience such a time of mourning and lamentation among a people. There were but few coloured [sic] people in the neighborhood—the most of my congregation was white.[51]

American Evangelical histories have often used character-focused narratives to tell the story of early Evangelicalism but have tended to spotlight white males.[52] Where are the texts that describe the rise of Evangelicalism through Black Evangelicals of the period, such as Harry Hoosier, George Liele, or Absalom Jones? This type of historiography produces a skewed picture of early Evangelicalism regarding its diversity and theology. Notwithstanding, the issue of recounting early African American Christianity has frequently been a question of sources. Illustrating this, historian Daniel Boorstin in "Invisible Communities: The Negroes' Churches" asserted:

---

[51] Richard Allen, *The Life, Experience, and Gospel Labors of the Rt. Rev. Richard Allen* (Philadelphia, PA: Martin & Boden, Printers, 1833), 9–10.

[52] For example, Mark Noll, *The Rise of Evangelicalism: The Age of Edwards, Whitefield, and the Wesleys* (Downers Grove, IL: IVP Academic, 2003).

[O]rganized white churches did not encompass the religious life of the Southern Negro. The Negro developed a religious life of his own. Much of this life remained *unrecorded* because many of the independent Negro religious meetings were illegal, and most of their participants, including sometimes even the preacher, were illiterate. Still we do know that such religious meetings were not uncommon, and that they became the nucleus, and later the whole organized form, of Negro communities. The Negroes' religious life thrived in institutions that were often invisible to the white masters, and that are barely visible to the historian today.[53]

However, Boorstin, like many early nineteenth-century American historians, ignored the slave narratives and other antebellum Black literary productions such as Black spiritual autobiographies and biographies, pamphlets, protest literature, sermons, and Black theological works from the period, which provide written insight into early African American Christianity. Moreover, the great majority of this literature was produced in an Evangelical milieu and theological thought-world, which is potentially bountiful, if included, for historians of American Evangelicalism. As Raboteau noted, by the early 1800s, Evangelicalism was the "predominant voice on the American religious scene," and Blacks, slave and free, expressed their faith and theology through this tradition.[54] Although historians of early American religion have come to incorporate more data from slave sources, historians of early American Evangelicalism have not exhibited such intersectionality despite the rise of Evangelicalism coinciding with the rise of the Black church in America.

---

[53] Daniel J. Boorstin, "Invisible Communities: The Negroes' Churches" in *The Americans: The National Experience* (New York: Random House, Vintage Books, 1965), 196–97, as quoted in Raboteau, *Slave Religion: The 'Invisible Institution' in the Antebellum South* (NY: Oxford University Press, 1978, 2004), x, emphasis mine.

[54] Raboteau, "Black Experience in American Evangelicalism," 92.

Perhaps this is because when one surveys how antebellum Blacks expressed Evangelicalism, it is not identical to that of white expression. As Raboteau said,

> The existence of chattel slavery in a nation that claimed to be Christian, and the use of Christianity to justify enslavement, confronted Black Evangelicals with a basic dilemma, which may be most clearly formulated in two questions: What meaning did Christianity, if it were a white man's religion, as it seemed, have for blacks; and why did the Christian God, if he were just as claimed, permit blacks to suffer so? In struggling to answer these questions, a significant number of Afro-Americans developed a *distinctive* evangelical tradition in which they established meaning and identity for themselves as individuals and as people. Simultaneously, they made an indispensable contribution to the development of American Evangelicalism.[55]

When antebellum Black Evangelicals entered the picture, Evangelicalism's definition widened. While more historically accurate to the tradition's early years, incorporating this data interrupts how the white experience in early U.S. American Evangelicalism has served as a descriptive and definitive norm for the tradition's historiography. This points to a lacuna in U.S. American Evangelical studies, an absence of histories centered on people of color. The absence of histories that center the Black Evangelical experience, especially in the tradition's formative years, is the third contributing factor to the modern disassociation of African American Christianity from Evangelicalism. It has overwhelmingly been defined historiographically through a paradigm of whiteness.

---

[55] Raboteau, "Black Experience in American Evangelicalism," 91–92, emphasis mine.

Incorporating in American Evangelical historiography what scholars of religion and historians have seen as the "distinct" Evangelical tradition that antebellum Blacks created will lessen this disassociation and offer a broader view of the Evangelical tradition and its theology. Furthermore, for the historian and theologian, a way of tracing a fundamental aspect of African American Christianity's root system is contributed. In other words, it tells us something about early Black Christianity in America *and* the contemporary predominant orientation to Christianity that African Americans exhibit, which found its grounding in the antebellum Black Evangelical experience.

Examining how African Americans uniquely conveyed a religious tradition in the United States has been the purview of the discipline of African American religion. As Glaude explains in his pragmatic approach to the discipline,

> The adjective refers . . . to a racial context within which religious meanings have been produced and reproduced. . . . The history of slavery and racial discrimination in the United States birthed particular religious formations among African Americans. African Americans converted to Christianity, for example, in the context of slavery. Many left predominantly white denominations to form their own after experiencing racial proscription and in pursuit of a sense of self-determination. Some embraced a distinctive interpretation of Islam to make sense of their condition in the United States. Given that history, we can reasonably and accurately describe certain variants of Christianity and Islam as African American and mean something beyond the rather uninteresting claim that black individuals belong to these different religious traditions.[56]

---

[56] Eddie Glaude, Jr., *African American Religion: A Very Short Introduction* (New York: Oxford University Press, 2014), 86. For a fuller treatment, see Eddie Glaude, Jr., *An Uncommon Faith: A Pragmatic Approach to the Study of African American Religion* (Athens, GA: The University of Georgia Press, 2018).

An interdisciplinary approach between the fields of American Evangelical history and African American religion will help illuminate the distinctiveness of the Black Evangelical experience, which I will refer to as *Afro-Evangelicalism*.[57] Peering into the antebellum world, which birthed Evangelicalism and African American Christianity, I will briefly explore two areas of distinction; namely, how African Americans interpreted the Gospel in Afro-Evangelicalism and the tradition's understanding of the character of God—both of which stood as separating points from their white counterparts.

The Gospel in Afro-Evangelicalism

Black preachers within Afro-Evangelicalism, slave and free, in the South and North, shared with their broader milieu what Glaude calls a "common grammar of faith" with their white Evangelical brethren.[58] Their shared Evangelical orientation gave them common ground in how they related to their Christian faith and a similar way of interpreting Scripture regarding hermeneutical frameworks. This did not mean, however, that they did not recognize a pronounced difference between themselves and white antebellum Evangelicals. Sources from the South and North maintained this, as Blacks understood that their differences were not surface but penetrated fundamental beliefs, such as the scope and teleological purposes of the Gospel.

---

[57] The term "Afro-Evangelicalism" has much overlap in meaning with that of "Gospel Haymanot." We are both focusing on the traditional expression of African American Christianity that has held together orthodoxy and Black flourishing, without seeing the two as in conflict. This contrasts with "Black Theology" which has put orthodoxy and Black flourishing at odds with each other. I have chosen to use "Afro-Evangelicalism" for two reasons. One, my scholarly focus has been specifically on how the Evangelical tradition has operated among African American Christians in the antebellum periods, while Gospel Haymanot is not confined to the Evangelical tradition or my era of focus. Two, I have retained the term "Evangelical" because Black people outside of the U.S., such as those on the continent and in South America, have used the term self-descriptively and thus it is helpful for comparative diaspora studies. However, overall, "Afro-Evangelicalism" fits within the larger category of "Gospel Haymanot" and is gladly embraced.

[58] Raboteau quotes his former student, Eddie Glaude. See Raboteau, *Slave Religion*, 331.

In the South, as expected, Black Evangelicals had to be more covert in the way that they communicated this difference. The lips of a visiting Black Union soldier in Wilmington, North Carolina reveal a window into their world in the closing days of the Civil War. As an escaped slave himself and Methodist minister from the South, he was acutely aware of the way Southern Blacks had to camouflage the distinctions in their theology. At the opening of his sermon in a primarily Black Methodist Episcopal Church, he said,

> One week ago you were all slaves; now you are all free. (Uproarious screamings). Thank God the armies of the Lord and Gideon has triumphed and the Rebels have been driven back in confusion and scattered like chaff before the wind. (Amen! Hallelujah!) I listened to your prayers, but I did not hear a single prayer offered for the President of the United States or for the success of the American [Union] Army. But I knew what you meant. You were not quite sure that you were free, therefore a little afraid to say boldly what you felt. *I know how it is. I remember how we used to have to employ dark symbols and obscure figures to cover up our real meaning. The profoundest philosopher could not understand us.*[59]

Blacks often utilized language that was ambiguous to outside ears because their interpretation of the Gospel did not fit the script white preachers endorsed. Without the guise of uniformity, slave preachers and pastors would have had no access to other slaves who were under the watchful eyes of white pastors and slave owners. Nevertheless, they found ways to navigate these troubled waters, as Anderson Edwards communicated. Speaking about his time as an enslaved preacher, he said,

---

[59] Lingurn Skidmore Burkhead, "History of the Difficulties of the Pastorate of the Front Street Methodist Church, Wilmington, N.C., for the Year 1865," *Historical Papers of the Trinity College Historical Society* (Durham, NC: Historical Society of Trinity College, 1908–9), 42, emphasis mine.

> I been preaching the gospel and farming since slavery time. I jined the church 'most 83 years ago when I was Major Gaud's slave, and they baptizes me in the spring branch close to where I finds the Lord. When I starts preaching I couldn't read or write and had to preach what Master told me, and he say tell them niggers iffen they obeys the master they goes to Heaven; *but I knowed there's something better for them, but daren't tell them 'cept on the sly. That I done lots. I tells 'em iffen they keeps praying, the Lord will set 'em free.*[60]

While not all white preachers in the South reduced the essential message of the Gospel to servile obedience to masters, Edwards' incorporation of *freedom* or *liberation* within his preaching was a commonly incorporated aspect of Black Evangelical interpretation of the Gospel that became a mainstay in Afro-Evangelicalism in a way that it did not for white Evangelicals. Conversely, liberation was a short-lived aspect of the Gospel for white Evangelicals living in the U.S. during the Revolutionary War: "During the Revolution ministers delighted in sermon texts which dealt with Israel's struggle for liberty against Pharaoh, and in celebrations of victory through the 1780s they likewise spoke repeatedly of Moses leading the people out of Egyptian bondage."[61] Therefore, it was not uncommon for ministers to echo the convictions of Congregationalist John Mellen in proclaiming that "liberty is the spirit and genius, not only of the gospel but the whole of that revelation, we have first and last, received from God."[62]

Nonetheless, when the fires of revolution cooled, *crucicentrism* became the primary interpretive lens for white Evangelicals,

---

[60] B. A. Botkin, *Lay My Burden Down: A Folk History of Slavery* (New York: Dell Publishing, 1973), 35, emphasis mine.
[61] Nathan O. Hatch, *The Sacred Cause of Liberty* (New Haven, CT: Yale University Press, 1977), 109.
[62] John Mellen, *The Great and Happy Doctrine of Liberty* (Boston, MA: Samuel Hall, 1795), 9; Hatch, *Sacred Cause of Liberty*, 157–158.

abolitionist and proslavery alike, to articulate the Gospel. David Bebbington has provided Evangelical studies with a frequently cited essential quadrilateral of characteristics describing this tradition. He has stated:

> There are the four qualities that have been the special marks of Evangelical religion: *conversionism*, the belief that lives need to be changed; *activism*, the expression of the gospel in effort; *biblicism*, a particular regard for the Bible; and what may be called *crucicentrism*, a stress on the sacrifice of Christ on the cross. Together, they form a quadrilateral of priorities that is the basis of Evangelicalism.[63]

Crucicentrism has been an organizing paradigm for understanding the meaning and purpose of the Gospel in the Western Christian tradition—Roman Catholic and early Protestant—setting it apart from the Orthodox churches. For Evangelicals, the crucicentric interpretation of the Gospel focused God's soteriological purposes around escaping the wrath of God because of humanity's sins. Antebellum Evangelicalism began in the wake of the early centuries that followed the Protestant Reformation. Although focuses on the "new birth" and "assurance of salvation" were developments characteristic of nascent Evangelicalism, the tradition carried within it the Reformation's central distinguishing doctrinal tenet, which was "justification by faith alone," an understanding that severed the salvific relationship between faith and works. Funneled into Evangelical preaching, the primary purpose of the Gospel, which African Americans received, was to facilitate the forgiveness of sins that could not come about through works or any other means but by appropriating Christ's work on the cross. Though voiced in varying ways, Black Evangelicals unquestionably received

---

[63] David Bebbington, *Evangelicalism in Modern Britain: A History from the 1730s to the 1980s* (New York: Routledge, 2005), 2.

and propagated this Gospel interpretation. The earliest spiritual biographies and slave narratives Blacks produced pointedly reveal this. For instance, George Liele, a former slave turned missionary, reflected this outlook when speaking of his conversion to Christianity: "I found no way wherein I could escape the damnation of hell, only through the merits of my dying Lord and Saviour [*sic*] Jesus Christ; which caused me to make intercession with Christ, for the salvation of my poor immortal soul."[64] Recounting her conversion to Christianity and joining Richard Allen's African Methodist Church, Jarena Lee recorded in her memoir that "as soon as the service closed he invited such as felt a desire to flee the wrath to come, to unite on trial with them—I embraced the opportunity."[65]

This aspect of Evangelicalism's Gospel made it a widely encompassing tradition. Rich and poor, Black and white, slave and free, could embrace it. However, as Afro-Evangelicalism matured, their sense of God's soteriological purposes in the Gospel widened beyond crucicentrism. There was an implicit expectation and emphasis that God's purposes in the coming of Jesus Christ were not only to facilitate the forgiveness of sins or escape the "wrath to come" but *also* to defeat the power of evil at work in the world that found its greatest manifestation through evil human actions, especially oppression and slavery. Articulating this perspective, formerly enslaved preacher Francis Grimke preached,

> In spite of the shallowness and emptiness and glaring hypocrisy of this thing which calls itself the church, this thing which is so timid, so cowardly that it dares not touch any sin that is unpopular, I still believe that Christianity is in this land. Today

---

[64] George Liele et al. "Letters Showing the Rise and Progress of the Early Negro Churches of Georgia and the West Indies," *The Journal of Negro History* 1, no. 1 (1916): 70.

[65] Jarena Lee, *The Religious Experience and Journal of Mrs. Jarena Lee: Giving an Account of Her Call to Preach the* Gospel (Philadelphia, PA: Published and Printed for the Author, 1849), 3–4.

it is like a little grain of mustard seed, but it has entered the soil, has germinated, and is springing up. It is like the little lump of leaven which the woman hid in three measures of meal: but it has begun to work, and will go on working, diffusing itself, until the whole is leavened. God has promised to give to his Son the heathen for his inheritance, and the uttermost parts of the earth for his possession: and in that promise this land is included. Christianity shall one day have sway even in Negro-hating America; the spirit which it inculcates, and which it is capable of producing, is sure, sooner or later, to prevail . . . I will not see it, you will not see it, but it is coming all the same. In the growth of Christianity, true, real, genuine Christianity in this land, I see the promise of better things for us as a race.[66]

While Black Evangelicals articulated this view through Protestant language, their expectations of the Gospel had implicit accentuations present within ancient Christianity. This leaning towards a wider soteriological lens that deals with the defeat of evil, the larger Christian tradition called *Christus Victor*. Though present in the early Church, this paradigm has remained the consistent organizing structure for articulating the Gospel in Orthodox Christianity. As Greek Orthodox theologian Stephen De Young explains, a significant problem in God's world is humanity's enslavement to the "dark principalities and powers," which Christ came to solve.[67] Moreover, as Anthony Balcomb points out in "Evangelicalism in Africa," this inclination was incorporated into African Evangelicalism as Africans struggled with apartheid and oppression.[68] When one views Evangelicalism through the

---

[66] Carter G. Woodson, ed., *The Works of Francis Grimke*, vol. 1, *Addresses Mainly Personal and Racial* (Washington, DC: The Associated Publishers Inc, 1942), 269–270.
[67] Stephen De Young, *The Religion of the Apostles: Orthodox Christianity in the First Century* (Chesterton, ID: Ancient Faith Publishing, 2021), 88.
[68] Anthony Balcomb, "Evangelicalism in Africa: What It Is and What It Does," in *Missionalia* 44, no. 2 (2016): 117–128. See his references to Nicholas Bhengu.

lens of the Black experience with oppression, Bebbington's crucicentrism does not fit the whole of the tradition.

The white Evangelical tradition in the antebellum period highly valued the transformation of human behavior to become more Christ-like. However, it was placed in the category of Christian ethics rather than soteriology and ambiguously defined throughout the tradition. Thus, in this arena, Afro-Evangelicalism came to two conclusions that differentiated it from its white counterpart. One, people who embraced enslavement to the "dark powers and principalities" at work in humanity's evil—in their context, slavery and oppression—could not truly be considered Christian. Secondly, Afro-Evangelicalism concluded that a part of God's soteriological purposes in the Gospel was liberation for the oppressed. Literature from Black Evangelicals in this period came to repeat this sentiment, as found in David Walker's *Appeal to the Colored Citizens of the World*, where he referred to "the white *Christians* of America, who hold us in slavery" as "pretenders to Christianity."[69] Further illustrative of this is the slave narrative of Louis Hughes. Slaveholding Christianity was oxymoronic to him. He declared,

> While my master showed these virtues [of talking of his slaves as he would cattle], similar to those which a provident farmer would show in the care of his dumb brutes, he lacked in that humane feeling which should have kept him from buying and selling human beings and parting kindred—which should have made it impossible for him to have permitted the lashing, beating and lacerating of his slaves, much more the hiring of an irresponsible brute, by the year, to perform this barbarous service for him. The McGees [his masters] were charitable—as they interpreted the word—were always ready to contribute

---

[69] David Walker, *"One Continual Cry": David Walker's Appeal to the Colored Citizens of the World,* ed. by Herbert Aptheker. (New York: Humanities Press, 1965), 62.

to educational and missionary funds, while denying, under the severest penalties, all education to those most needing it, and all true missionary effort—the spiritual enlightenment for which they were famishing. Then our masters lacked that fervent charity, the love of Christ in the heart, which if they had possessed they could not have treated us as they did.[70]

The oxymoronic view Afro-Evangelicalism developed towards slaveholding Christianity not only pointed to a difference in understanding regarding the scope of the Gospel but the character of God as well. Leading up to the Civil War, white Evangelical denominations split over the issue of slavery. However, in the wake of Reconstruction, as they began to mend their wounds, both sides were quiet about Southern violence towards Blacks after the war. With Afro-Evangelicalism, Blacks free and formerly enslaved still looked to a God whose Gospel they believed would lead to their liberation and, if accepted by whites, would release them from their slavery to oppression.

---

[70] Louis Hughes, *Thirty Years a Slave* (Milwaukee, WI: South Side Printing Company, 1897), 189.

Horus and Jesus: Similarities, Differences, and Their Implications

Erika Brown

Introduction

Within the realm of social media discourse, it is a common assertion that the narrative accounts of Jesus Christ documented in the New Testament are essentially a reimagining of the mythical accounts of the ancient Egyptian deity Horus. Horus was indeed a prominent deity in ancient Egypt, with his worship dating back to as early as the Predynastic period, which predates the written history of ancient Egypt. He was one of the most significant and enduring gods in the Egyptian pantheon. Horus's iconic imagery, including the falcon-headed representation, can be found in various Egyptian contexts, including tombs, jewelry, coffins, and other artifacts. His role as a god of protection and divine kingship made him a central figure in ancient Egyptian religious beliefs and practices. Because Jesus Christ is the central figure of the Christian faith, some employ the claim of Horus's reimagining to question the historicity of the biblical accounts and, consequently, the Christian faith itself. Indeed, this argument is not a new one; it has existed in various forms over the years. However, its resurgence and newfound popularity can largely be attributed to its frequent regurgitation across social media platforms. What is most alarming about these arguments, whether for or against, is that they are frequently advanced without any reference or citation of credible data or sources. Even more alarming is that, despite the absence of references or citations to reliable data or sources, these claims continue to be unquestioningly embraced within the realm of social media.

Given the new prevalence and apparent persuasiveness of this argument, it seems imperative to revisit and reengage this topic through a comprehensive analysis of the available ancient texts and archaeological data relating to this particular topic. While this topic consists of numerous contestable elements, this paper will center its analysis on two essential components inherent to the narratives of both Jesus Christ and Horus: miraculous births and deaths/resurrections. The goal of this paper is to demonstrate that a detailed and thorough exploration of the available ancient texts and archaeological data, will demonstrate that the Horus myth and the Gospel accounts of Jesus Christ, despite their importance within their respective traditions, retain distinct identities that differentiate them from one another completely. Moreover, this paper will serve as a demonstration of the advantages of engaging with ancient artifacts and texts when discussing ancient contexts and/or beliefs.

Data: Miraculous Birth Accounts

The accounts of Jesus Christ's conception and birth are documented in the canonical texts of the New Testament Gospels of Matthew and Luke. According to Luke 1:26–38, the conception of Jesus Christ was initially announced to the virgin mother of Jesus, Mary (Luke 1:34).[71] The announcement also came separately to Mary's betrothed husband, Joseph, in Matthew 1:18–23. The accounts emphasize that Mary's pregnancy was a result of the intervention of the Holy Spirit, and it is explicitly stated that she remained a virgin both during the

---

[71] Mary's virginity can also be assumed based upon Matt. 1:18.

conception process and the eventual birth of Jesus, as indicated in Luke 1:34–35 and Matthew 1:24–25. In highlighting Mary's virginity, both texts utilize the biblically common sexual euphemism "knowing a man" ἄνδρα οὐ γεινώσκω (Luke 1:34) and οὐκ ἐγίνωσκεν (Matthew 1:24). In Luke, the word utilized to describe the process of Jesus' conception, ἐπέρχομαι, means "to come to" or "to draw near." It is important to note that this term, whether found in biblical or extrabiblical contexts, has never been employed with a sexual connotation. This fact underscores the absence of any mentions of sexual activity within this particular narrative. Hence, the conception of Jesus Christ was a miraculous occurrence, as it occurred without any form of sexual interaction between the virgin Mary and the Holy Spirit.

While both Joseph and Mary hailed from Nazareth, the events surrounding the birth of Jesus Christ unfolded in Bethlehem, as detailed in Luke 2:4–6 and Matthew 2:1. The requirement to comply with a census led Joseph and the pregnant Mary to undertake the journey to Bethlehem (Luke 2:4). Upon their arrival, they found the area in Bethlehem to be crowded, which resulted in significantly limited hospitality space as is evident in Luke 2:7. As a matter of fact, the Greek text referring to this limitation reads διότι οὐκ ἦν αὐτοῖς τόπος ἐν τῷ κατ αλύματι, which should be understood to mean that there was no room in the "guest room" as opposed to "inn." The unavailability of the guest room typically available in ancient Palestinian dwellings meant that the only space available to Joseph and the pregnant Mary was the stable area. Furthermore, the circumstances and location of his birth serves as an explanation for the placement of a newborn Jesus in a manger (Luke 2:7). It is essential to note that neither Gospel account specifies a particular calendar date or season for Jesus's birth. There is only the mention in Luke that these events occurred during the period when Caesar Augustus ordered a census (Luke 2:1). Therefore, it is essential to recognize that the choice of December 25 as the associated date for the birth of Jesus Christ does not originate from the canonical sources themselves.

The accounts of the Egyptian god Horus's conception and birth are not contained within one singular canonical source. Instead, they are spread across various ancient Egyptian texts and artifacts. Oftentimes, the accounts pertaining to Horus vary and evolve over time, which is common in ancient mythology and religious traditions. One of the key sources that delves into the conception of Horus is located within the Coffin Texts. The Coffin Texts are a collection of Egyptian funerary magical formulas found on the interior and/or exterior of Egyptian coffins dating to the Middle Kingdom period. Coffin Text Spell 148 is featured on eight coffins dating between 2130–1630 BCE.[72] In the opening sequence of Spell 148, the Egyptian goddess and sister-wife of the god Osiris, Isis, merely finds that she is pregnant with Horus. Lines 209–210 read, "Taking shape as a falcon. The lightning-flash strikes (?), the gods are afraid, Isis wakes pregnant with the seed of her brother Osiris. She is uplifted, (even she) the widow, and her heart is glad with the seed of her brother Osiris."[73]

In the lines that follow, her pregnancy is subsequently revealed to the other deities. Although Spell 148 alludes to her pregnancy, it fails to provide clear details about the way in which her conception took place. In this context, her pregnancy becomes evident only after the occurrence of lightning strikes. Fortunately, more comprehensive accounts of Horus's conception can be found in the Pyramid Texts. The Pyramid Texts, which predate the Coffin Texts, also consist of a collection of funerary magical formulas. Pyramid Text 366, attributed

---

[72] "There are 8/7 known copies S2C^a, S2C^b on the outer coffin and S1C^a, S1C^b on the inner coffin of *Msht* at Siut. These are very poorly preserved. There is also B4C which is found on the outer coffin of *S3t-nd* at El-Bersheh. Finally copies of the spell are S1Chass, S1P, S2P which are found on the inner and outer coffins of *Nhti* at Siut. All these copies show evidence that the texts were all reproduced by a different scribe while the spell was either recited from memory or orally read from a master copy." See Robert H. O'Connell, "The Emergence of Horus: An Analysis of Coffin Text Spell 148," in *The Journal of Egyptian Archaeology* 69, no. 1 (1983): 66.

[73] Mordechai Gilula, "Coffin Texts Spell 148," *The Journal of Egyptian Archaeology* 57 (1971): 14.

to Pharaoh Teti of Dynasty VI (2323–2291 BCE), and 518, attributed to Pharaoh Pepi I of Dynasty VI (ca. 2289–2255 BCE), offer more details relating to Isis's impregnation. Pyramid Text 366 reads, "Your sister Isis has come to you, aroused [for] love of you. You have put her on your phallus so that your seed might emerge into her, sharp as Sothis, and sharp Horus has emerged from you as Horus in Sothis."[74] Pyramid Text 518 reads,

> So, stand up, Osiris, and commend this Pepi to those over the causeway "Sound of Heart," north of the Marsh of Rest, like you commended Horus to Isis on the day you impregnated her, that they may let Pepi eat from the marshes and drink from the springs inside the Marsh of Rest.[75]

While Pyramid Text 518 identifies Osiris as an active participant in Isis's impregnation, Pyramid Text 366 details Isis's participation in Osiris's sexual arousal and then their subsequent sexual intercourse. A more elaborate description of Isis's impregnation is documented in the "Great Hymn of Osiris" from the Amenmose Stele of Dynasty XVIII (1539–1292 BCE). A segment of the stele reads,

> Isis the beneficent, the one who protects her brother, who searches for him without tiring, who travels this country in his mourning; she did not stop before having found him. It is she who casts shadow on him with her feathers, air with her wings, who performs the rites of jubilation and has her brother buried . . . It is she who raises up what is collapsed in the god with a failing heart, who extracts his seed, who procreates an heir.[76]

---

[74] James P. Allen, *The Ancient Egyptian Pyramid Texts* (Atlanta, GA: Society of Biblical Literature, 2005), 81.
[75] Allen, *Pyramid Texts*, 159–160.
[76] Translation, "Arched Stele; Stele with Two Registers" limestone stele, Louvre, Paris, accessed October 20, 2023, https://collections.louvre.fr/en/ark:/53355/cl010026515.

Based upon these accounts, it is apparent that Isis's pregnancy resulted from her "extracting his [Osiris's] seed" and it is then that Isis "procreates an heir [Horus]." Another important source is *Concerning Isis and Osiris*, a later collection of the Egyptian mythological accounts of Isis and Osiris, by the Greek historian and biographer Plutarch (46–120 AD). This text claims that Isis recovered the scattered body parts of the murdered Osiris and copulated with his restored "member," i.e., his phallus, and became pregnant with Horus.[77]

Depictions of the "conception of Horus" have also been uncovered at ancient temples located in Abydos and Dendera. At Abydos, in the New Kingdom temple of Seti I (c.1290–1279 BCE), depictions were found on the south (east) wall of the Ptah-Sokar Chapel. David O'Conner provides a detailed description of this relief:

> [T]he murdered, dismembered but reassembled Osiris is shown lying on a bier. His consort, the goddess Isis, descends in the form of a kite onto his erect phallus, which has been defaced. As a result, Isis will give birth to Osiris' son Horus, who also stands at the foot of the bier, while his mother, Isis, stands at the head. In the atemporal divine world, deities can appear multiple times in the same scene.[78]

There are three separate depictions of Horus's conception in Dendera at the temple of Hathor, which dates to the Greco-Roman

---

[77] Plutarch, "De Iside et Osiride," in *Moralia*, trans. Frank Cole Babbitt, §18, §19, and §38, (Cambridge: Harvard University, 1936) http://www.perseus.tufts.edu/hopper/text?doc=Perseus%3Atext%3A2008.01.0239.

[78] Lloyd Graham, "From Isis-kite to Nekhbet-vulture and Horus-falcon: Changes in the Identification of the Bird above Osiris's Phallus in Temple 'Conception of Horus' Scenes, *Birmingham Egyptology Journal* 8 no. 1 (2020–21): 1–32, https://more.bham.ac.uk/birminghamegyptology/birmingham-egyptology-journal/volume-8-2020-21-birmingham-egyptology-journal/.

period (ca. 52–25 BCE).[79] The first scene is located on the east wall of the innermost room of the eastern chapels. The remaining two are located within the innermost room of the western Osiris chapels on the east and west walls, respectively.[80] All three contain depictions much like the relief described above, that is, of a deceased, mummified Osiris lying atop a bier with his consort Isis hovering above his erect phallus in the form of a kite. These depictions serve as a great visual aid to the account of Horus's conception as recorded in the "the Great Hymn of Osiris" discussed above. Based upon both the texts and depictions discussed, it is evident that the conception of Horus was a posthumous conception resulting from sexual intercourse between Isis and the deceased Osiris. Furthermore, given the wide range of dates for the recording of this account, it is also evident that this was the standard belief regarding Horus's conception for thousands of years.

Several ancient Egyptian texts reference the birth of Horus, yet the majority simply note the occurrence of his birth without providing specific details about the events surrounding it. One of the primary sources for the account of Horus's birth is the Ancient Egyptian Magical Spell 90 (AEMT 90). This spell is featured (either whole or partial) on the following artifacts: Metternich Stela (Cippus of Horus) dated to 360–343 BCE; the Socle Béhague (ca. third century BCE), (3) Horus cippi in Cairo, Leiden, and Baltimore; (2) statues guerisseuses in Paris and Beirut; and P. Hay 9961 (fourth century BCE or earlier).[81] According to AEMT 90, Horus's birth occurred at Khemmis, an ancient city situated in the Delta region of ancient Egypt. The events of his birth unfolded while Isis sought protection from Seth, the Egyptian god and

---

[79] Graham, "From Isis-kite," 6. It should be noted that Graham suggests that maybe one of these depictions were not Isis or possibly that one of the depictions should not be understood to be a phallus.
[80] Graham, "From Isis-kite," 13.
[81] Graham, "From Isis-kite," 78.

nemesis of Osiris.[82] Seth had already murdered Isis's brother-husband Osiris and was seeking to kill Osiris's son and heir, Horus. Thoth, the Egyptian god of the moon, recommended that Isis "conceal herself with the young boy Horus. Isis fled to Khemmis, at the edge of the Nile Delta. Then a poor marsh-girl who lived nearby opened her hovel and welcomed Isis. In this hovel, she subsequently gave birth to Horus. It should be noted that there is some debate as to whether this spell speaks to Isis being pregnant with Horus or whether Horus is merely a young child already.[83] However, the prevailing view among scholars is that this account involves a pregnant Isis.

Coffin Text Spells 286, 474, 480, and 989 offer additional details relating to events of Horus's birth. According to Spell 286, not only was Horus born in Khemmis, but he was also nursed in the Field of Fire when he was received on the birth-stool. In Spells 474 and 480, Isis is the one who cuts her own naval cord following the birth of Horus. Spell 989 notes that Horus was born "within the god's tamarisk." The term "tamarisk" (or "tamarix") refers to a type of plant or shrubbery frequently cited in ancient Near Eastern texts. This botanical reference likely elucidates the recurrent depiction of the infant Horus among marshes and plant bushes.

Like the birth accounts of Jesus Christ, the narratives of Horus's birth do not specify a date within the accounts themselves. The precise dating of the ancient celebration of Horus's birth remains unclear. Currently, the sole ancient source mentioning any type of celebration comes from the Greek writer Plutarch. According to Plutarch, the celebration of Horus's birth occurred "about the time of the winter solstice [when] she gave birth to Harpocrates, imperfect

---

[82] *Ancient Egyptian Magical Texts*, trans. J. F. Borghouts, in Religious Texts Translations Series, vol. 9 (Leiden: Brill, 1978), 62–63.

[83] Lloyd Graham, "From Isis and Horus in the Delta to Mary and Jesus in Ireland," in *Göttinger Miszellen: Beiträge zur ägyptologischen Diskussion,* 265 (Göttingen: Göttinger Miszellen, 2016): 79.

and premature, amid the early flowers and shoots."[84] However, no other ancient Egyptian artifact or text has been identified to corroborate this information.

Death and Resurrection

The death and resurrection of Jesus Christ is recorded in all four canonical Gospels of the New Testament: Matthew 26:14–28:15, Mark 14:43–16:12, Luke 22:47–24:50, and John 18:1–20:29. According to these Gospel accounts, Jesus was betrayed and arrested (Matthew 26:47–56; Mark 14:43–52; Luke 22:47–53; John 18:1–11), endured a cumbersome and questionable trial process (Matthew 27:1–26; Mark 15:1–15; Luke 22:66–23:24; John 18:28–19:16), and endured Roman flogging and a Roman crucifixion (Matthew 27:32–46; Mark 15:21–25; Luke 23:26–46; John 19:16–30). He was then buried in the tomb of a wealthy Jewish man (Matthew 27:57–61; Mark 15:42–47; Luke 23:50–56; John 19:38–42) and came back to life after three days inside of the sealed tomb (Matthew 28:1–7; Mark 16:1; Luke 24:1–12; John 20:1–9).

Regarding the death and resurrection of Horus, AEMT 90 is the primary account detailing these events. According to AEMT 90, Horus, as a child, was brought back to life by his mother Isis after being stung by a scorpion. There is some debate about whether the translation indicates his death or him being near death. However, the account does not specify the duration of his state, whether dead or near death, nor does it mention any form of burial. It only records that his mother, Isis, was the one who magically revived him. In terms of depictions, the majority tend to portray a young, resurrected Horus among a large variety of animals, such as oryxes, snakes, or lions and scorpions. However, scorpions are clearly the primary focus of the spell.[85] Otherwise, there are no known depictions of his death and

---

[84] Plutarch, *De Iside et Osiride*, §65. Harpocrates is the Greek equivalent for Horus.
[85] Marie Vandenbeusch, "Evidence of an Ancient Archive? The Papyrus British Museum EA 9961," *The Journal of Egyptian Archaeology* 104, no. 2 (2018), 189.

subsequent resurrection. The scarcity of accounts or depictions related to this narrative may be attributed to its non-essential nature within the myth. Apart from this specific account, there are no other known narratives detailing Horus's death, and consequently, there is no mention of his resurrection as an adult deity.

Discussion

Upon a cursory examination of the data presented above, it becomes increasingly evident just how distinct the narratives of Jesus Christ and the Egyptian god Horus are from one another. Both stories involve miraculous conceptions, but the methods of impregnation differ significantly. In the case of Mary, her impending pregnancy is first privately announced to her and her betrothed husband, after which she is miraculously impregnated non-sexually through the Spirit of God merely "coming upon her." In contrast, Isis receives no such announcement about an impending pregnancy. In one account, Isis is simply discovered to be pregnant, while in a more detailed narrative, she actively brings about her pregnancy or becomes pregnant through posthumous intercourse with Osiris.

It is also crucial to realize that Osiris and Isis are consistently depicted as a married couple. As a matter of fact, ancient Egyptian cultural expressions of copulation often symbolized the metaphorical nature of the connection between Osiris and Isis.[86] Therefore, even in a scenario of a non-sexual conception of Horus, Isis cannot be regarded as a virgin due to her prior intimate relationship with Osiris. Notably, in the context of a non-sexual conception of Horus, it is inaccurate to consider Isis a virgin, given her historical involvement with her husband and the symbolic representations of their relationship in Egyptian culture. On the other hand, the New Testament Gospel accounts highlight the virgin conception of Jesus, emphasizing Mary's purity and

---

[86] Maria Rosa Valdesogoi, "Everyday Images, Resurrection Metaphors," *Lumen Et Virtus: Revista Interdisciplinar De Cultura E Imagem* 12, no. 30 (2021): 60–76.

the miraculous nature of the event. This is reinforced by the absence of explicit details on sexual activity.

The birthing accounts also reveal distinctive features. Both involved relocations, but the circumstances of the relocations differed significantly. Mary and Joseph's relocation was prompted by non-hostile factors, specifically compliance with a government census. However, the overcrowded city led to the unavailability of a "guest room," compelling Mary to give birth to Jesus Christ in the stable area in Bethlehem. In contrast, Isis relocated to Khemmis to evade the threat of murder by Seth, and it was in this location that Horus was born, amid some type of marsh or bush.

It is important to note that none of the previously examined accounts pinpoint December 25 or any closely associated date as the birth date for either Jesus Christ or Horus. Concerning Jesus Christ's birth date, early Christian speculation abounded, with figures like the early church father Clement of Alexandria (150–215 CE) being cited for saying,

> There are those who have calculated not only the year of our Lord's birth, but also the day. They say that it took place in the twenty-eighth year of Augustus, on the twenty-fifth day of Pachon [May 20] ... Others say that He was born on the twenty-fourth or twenty-fifth day of Pharmuthi [April 19 or 20].[87]

However, by the third and fourth centuries CE, December 25 became the established celebrated date for Jesus Christ's birth, as evidenced in the works of Christian author Hippolytus of Rome and the *Apostolic Constitutions*.[88] The origins of this date as the chosen day for Christ's birth remain a subject of much debate. It is clear that the

---

[87] *Dictionary of Early Christian Beliefs: A Reference Guide to More Than 700 Topics Discussed by the Early Church Fathers*, ed. David W. Bercot (Peabody, MA: Hendrickson Publishers, 2021), s.v. "Birth of Jesus."
[88] *Dictionary of Early Christian Beliefs*, s.v. "Calendar, Christian."

association of December 25 with the birth of Christ is a product of cultivated traditions rather than a direct designation from the original accounts themselves. Similarly, the celebration of Horus's birth around the winter solstice, as documented by Plutarch, underscores that this dating for the celebration did not necessarily originate in earlier ancient contexts, nor was it likely consistently practiced.

The narratives surrounding the deaths and resurrections of Jesus Christ and Horus are equally distinct, mirroring the disparities observed in their birthing accounts. Both were innocent in their deaths, but the similarities end there. Jesus Christ, an adult man presumably in his early thirties, endured a traumatic death process that included severe flogging and culminated in Roman crucifixion. Following his death, Jesus Christ was entombed for three days before being miraculously resurrected by the power of God. In contrast, the death of Horus occurred during his infancy or childhood. His death was attributed to mere poisoning from a scorpion bite. After his death, Horus was then resurrected to life through the magical power of his mother, Isis. As stated above, aside from this account, there are no known accounts of the death and subsequent resurrection of the adult deity Horus. Curiously, it is Osiris, the adult deity and father of Horus, who undergoes both death and resurrection. While Horus was not necessarily an active participant in his own resurrection, he was an active participant in the resurrection of Osiris. Ultimately, these details serve to underscore the marked differences between the resurrection accounts of Horus and Jesus Christ.

Conclusion

Ultimately, the accounts of the conception, birth, death, and resurrection of Horus and Jesus Christ diverge significantly. A thorough and meticulous examination of both narratives reveals substantial distinctions that challenge the notion that the accounts of Jesus Christ are reimagined accounts of the mythical accounts of the

Egyptian deity Horus. Certainly, broad similarities do exist, but such resemblances do not necessarily imply inauthenticity. The repeated assertion of their "identical" nature lacks reliable evidence and all too often stems from a disregard for the archaeological materials relating to this subject.

The utilization of archaeological data plays a pivotal role in elucidating the distinct differences between the narratives of the Egyptian god Horus and Jesus Christ. The benefits of engaging with archaeological materials lie in their ability to provide tangible, contextually rich insights that transcend mere assertions. By delving into the foundational tenets and teachings of each story, archaeology enables a more comprehensive understanding of the historical and cultural contexts surrounding these narratives. This method not only challenges oversimplified claims but also fosters a nuanced appreciation for the unique aspects of each narrative. In the pursuit of truth and accuracy, archaeological data stands as a valuable tool, offering a tangible connection to the past and contributing to a more informed and authentic interpretation of these ancient narratives.

Reimagining the Historically Black Church's Missional Ecclesiology: Serving the Ger in Our Midst

Corey Lee

Introduction

Our world is changing at an ever-increasing pace. Globalization, climate change, regional conflicts, and other forces in the world have created unprecedented global movements across the world. Technology continues to shrink our world, transforming Earth into an increasingly diverse and pluralistic world. With so many things changing, people are searching for security. For Black people in the United States, the rock of their community has always been the Black Church.

"No pillar of the African-American community has been more central to its history, identity, and social justice vision than the 'Black Church.'"[89] Despite these profound words from Henry Louis Gates Jr. and the historical contributions of the Black Church to the Black community in the U.S., the Black Church faces a great crisis. Since the assassination of Martin Luther King Jr., the historically Black

---

[89] Henry Louis Gates, Jr., *The Black Church: This Is Our Story, This is Our Song* (New York: Penguin Press, 2021), 1.

Church has lost its prophetic vision and witness, instead becoming intoxicated by its own empowerment. Without a significant reversal, the Black Church may succumb to the growing influence of secularization, religious pluralism, and shifting community demographics. This paper will argue that the Black Church must recall its historical roots and connection to the Exodus tradition, remembering its former status as slave and stranger, to catalyze a movement from the Black Church's present place of empowerment to reimagine a new missional ecclesiology. This missional ecclesiology must serve immigrant populations and other people of color who are relocating to historically Black neighborhoods and communities surrounding historically Black Churches.

I will first situate myself as I approach this topic. Next, I will present the current state of the Black Church in the U.S. I will then introduce the Old Testament concept of the stranger (*ger*). Furthermore, I will connect the *ger* with the Black Church. Finally, I will conclude by illustrating what reimagining a new missional ecclesiology could look like among the Black Church today.

Situating Myself

I was born into a home in North Newton, Kansas and was formed by two young Black people from urban Kansas City. My parents were securely connected to and aware of their Black roots and all that entailed, having lived through the Civil Rights Movement and the assassination of Rev. Dr. Martin Luther King. Both came from unstable households that were stabilized by a strong village support system rooted in the Black Church. My father came from a long line of ministers in the Church of God in Christ, and my mother was from the Christian Methodist Episcopal Church.

Everything I have learned in life is in some way connected to my upbringing at Hall's Chapel, African Methodist Episcopal Church. From learning Black history that was not taught in a public school in

Newton, to socialization, public speaking, leadership, and intergenerational relationships, my life was anchored in the Black Church. This was a stabilizing force and place of refuge as I navigated the realities of being the only Black person in my class until middle school. Living in Kansas, I was called a "nigger" countless times, experienced racial profiling, and was the victim of police brutality as a teenager. I have been spat upon and told what I could not do because I was Black. Yet, it was the Black Church that gave me a different narrative. It was the Black Church that introduced me to Historically Black Colleges and Universities, shaped me to be an emerging leader, and grounded me when I tried to wild out during my college years. It was in a Black Church that I accepted my calling and started my journey to where I am today.

In view of being nurtured and raised by the Black Church, I write this paper to call forth current and emerging Black leaders to return to the Black Church reimagined. Many have been wounded by the Black Church, but the Black Church still has much to offer the Black community and other marginalized communities surrounding Black Churches. It is at this point that I now turn to a more in-depth survey of the current state of the Black Church.

The State of the Black Church in the U.S.

Walter E. Fluker says, "The memories of the past are no longer adequate to sustain the mission of black churches in these turbulent times. The little house in which we lived and made due cannot contain the new moments to which black churches are called . . . black churches' historical identity and agency have been stymied by the shifting grounds of a post-racial era, thus forfeiting their prophetic role in the world."[90] Furthermore, Fluker argues that Black churches need to determine whether they can effectively use race as an emancipatory

---

[90] Walter Fluker, *The Ground Has Shifted: The Future of the Black Church in Post-Racial America* (New York: New York University Press, 2016), 17.

instrument and offers ideas for the conjuring of new liberating practices for churches. In addition to noting the shifting foundations of the Black Church, Fluker re-stories the Black journey, exchanging the Exodus story for one of exile:

> The exilic predicament of African Americans provides fertile ground for theologizing about our relationship with other brothers and sisters in the many diasporas that populate our postcolonial world; it also confronts us with the question of our existential and aesthetic estrangement and the question of the "stranger" (maybe our other sisters and brothers from whom we have been "estranged").[91]

I am not ready to dismiss the Exodus narrative for Black people, especially considering figures comparable to Moses—Harriet Tubman and Martin Luther King Jr.—who both led exodus movements out of slavery and the Jim Crow South. I am interested in Fluker's question of the stranger as it is relevant to my research; the term "stranger" has implications for reimagining a new missional ecclesiology for the Black Church. This matter I will explore more thoroughly in the coming sections.

One of the greatest indicators that the ground has shifted for the Black Church is the Black Lives Matter Movement. For the first time, a major civil rights movement was pioneered without the leadership of pastors from the Black Church. Mantras like "this ain't your grandparent's civil rights movement,"[92] coined by rapper Tef Poe, illustrate the distance between the emerging generation of Black leaders and previous generations. Eboni Marshall Turman captures the deep pain many former Black Church attendees grapple with, stating, "The

---

[91] Fluker, *Ground Has Shifted*, 17.
[92] Oscar Blayton, "Ain't Your Grandparents' Civil Rights Movement," *The Washington Informer*, October 20, 2014, https://www.washingtoninformer.com/aint-your-grandparents-civil-rights-movement/.

Black Church has been the place where so many of us have come to know a God of justice and a God of love. . . . But it has simultaneously been a place that has wounded so many of us."[93] It is in this milieu of opportunity and controversy that Black churches and Black communities experienced both an economic explosion and a decline in relevance.

According to Henry Louis Gates Jr., "the affluent sought a different kind of fulfillment from their church home, with a focus on the welfare, needs, and anxieties of the individual."[94] This shift from a communal focus to an individualistic focus has serious implications. The new wealth explosion also paved the way for the growing Prosperity Gospel Movement. Originally meant to help Black people, it enslaved the "haves" to pursue excess while taking from the "have nots" what little they possessed. Fluker adds, "Possessive individualism is concentrated on capital and its promised, but elusive, rewards of recognition and prestige that perform a séance with race, religion, and culture, conjuring the ghostly entrancement of many of our church leaders who embody and speak for an 'unholy ghost.'"[95]

Before leaving the Black Church for a season, Thabiti Anyabwile lamented, "The institution that helped nurture me I now deem a real enemy to the progress of African Americans, an opiate, and a tool of white supremacy. I had experienced enough of the church's weakness to reject her altogether." Years later, reflecting on his younger self, Anyabwile reflected, "The immature and undiscerning rarely know how to handle the failures of its heroes, to evaluate with nuance and critical appreciation. That was true of me before the Lord saved me."[96] Fortunately for him, Christ found him and brought him back to the faith of his ancestors. Increasingly, his story is becoming

---

[93] Gates, *Black Church*, 158.
[94] Gates, *Black Church*, 170.
[95] Fluker, *Ground Has Shifted*, 17.
[96] Thabiti Anyabwile, *Reviving The Black Church: A Call to Reclaim a Sacred Institution* (Nashville, TN: B&H Publishing Group, 2015), 8.

less common. New trends among youth and young adults also perplexed church leaders. Growing discontent with traditional conservative values and lack of contextual expressions of their faith sent tremors through this demographic. Multitudes of the next generation have abandoned the faith of their ancestors to pursue religious others or no religion at all.

The final trend I want to highlight must be seen through the missional eyes of the Spirit. Massive forces of change and exploding global migration are reshaping the demographic landscapes around historically Black churches. Emmy-winning investigative reporter Alesandra Ram wrote, "While 'white flight' and the Civil Rights movement galvanized the Black community, 'Black flight' (middle-class African Americans relocating to the suburbs) and the rapid gentrification of neighborhoods across America have put the Black church on the path to obsoletion."[97] Social entrepreneur and rapper Amisho Baraka mirrors these sentiments in his song "My Hood USA," rapping, "Blacks move to the 'burbs tryna escape the system, but they took stability and wealth right along with 'em. Their ownership and financial stimulation, it makes it much easier for gentrification."[98] Ram and Lewis both articulate the evolving reality of Black communities that the Black Church must address. In addition to Black flight and gentrification, the world is experiencing unprecedented migration. Some are moving to access affordable living while others are moving to merely preserve living. There are several implications for the future of the Black Church concerning these disruptive changes. I dedicate the next section to the biblical responsibility of communities to care for newcomers in Black communities.

---

[97] Allesandra Ram, "In Changing Neighborhoods, Black Churches Face an Identity Crisis," *The Atlantic*, October 12, 2012, https://www.theatlantic.com/national/archive/2012/10/in-changing-neighborhoods-black-churches-face-an-identity-crisis/263305/.

[98] Amisho Baraka, "My Hood USA," featuring Vanessa Hill, by Amisho Baraka, track 11 on *The Narrative*, released October 10, 2016, posted December 12, 2016, by UrbanGospel TV, YouTube video, 4 min. 38 sec., https://www.youtube.com/watch?v=3SEWSeyeEFs.

Strangers in Our Midst

Welcoming outsiders into one's community with care and compassion has been a central theme in both the Old and New Testament canon. In the pages of the Pentateuch, Yahweh demonstrates His heart to protect those living in foreign lands and/or in positions of vulnerability. Abram experienced Yahweh's care as he traveled from Haran to his new home in Cannan. His life was an example and was referenced numerous times throughout Scripture. This section will explore the correlation between the definition of the Hebrew word for stranger (*ger*) in the Old Testament text and the Black Church's call to care for *ger* in the Black Church.

It is important to note the variety of meanings for *ger*. It applies to Israel in the days of Egyptian captivity and to their rise and deliverance through Moses. It refers to the people who met Yahweh on the mountain, the rise of their monarchy, and their eventual prosperous covenant-keeping nation. It also encompasses Israel as an exiled people who departed and returned to the promised land. Israel's tumultuous existence has contributed to the formation and evolution of the term *ger*. Initial examination of this term yields several sources that must be considered when developing a definition for the *ger*.

The Evolution of the Term Ger in Scripture

I have selected four passages of Scripture to research that help to capture the evolution of the term *ger*: Deuteronomy 24:14–22; 26:1–15; Leviticus 19:9–10, 33–34; 25:35–38. Deuteronomy is written as a summary of events. Moses is recorded admonishing Israel toward faithfulness to Yahweh. Richard Nelson says: "Deuteronomy's fundamental purpose of motivating obedience is disclosed in a frequently repeated line of reasoning: listen and obey so that you may benefit in the land."[99] Nelson further notes that Deuteronomy is etched in

---

[99] Richard D. Nelson, *Deuteronomy: A Commentary* (Louisville, KY: Westminster John Knox Press, 2002), 1.

the biblical canon as Moses's farewell address to Israel just prior to his death. It is important to note that Moses spoke as a *ger* to the people who were *gerim* in the land of Moab. Deuteronomy recounts Yahweh's intent to forge a just and humane society. He accomplished this by advocating for concrete measures to aid the vulnerable in Israel. Several times He uses Israel's sojourn as *ger* to imbue compassion in the heart of His people. Moses assumes a homiletical and didactic tone, directly exhorting Israel in second-person language. Nelson noted, "Incessant repetition aims for rhetorical effect and ease of retention."[100] Deuteronomy is Moses's last will and testament urging Israel to say yes to Yahweh.

Leviticus captures events between Israel's arrival and departure at Mount Horeb. Erhard S. Gerstenberger suggests Leviticus "consistently presupposes Israel's sojourn in Yahweh's proximity."[101] In Leviticus, the term *ger* is shaped in the context of intimacy with Yahweh. Additionally, as Gerstenberger points out, "Not a single chapter in this book has been composed in a single sweep or by a single hand."[102] Since there are numerous voices contributing to the meaning of the text, one must assume that those shaping voices meticulously crafted multiple definitions of the *ger* according to their context. Gerstenberger further posits, "[Leviticus] came about within the framework of an early Jewish (postexilic) worship."[103] This brief introduction of Deuteronomy and Leviticus provides a backdrop as to how the term *ger* was shaped in these sacred texts. At this point, I want to provide a brief exegetical analysis of the word *ger* using the four passages noted above.

---

[100] Nelson, *Deuteronomy*, 2.
[101] Erhard Gerstenberger, *Leviticus: A Commentary* (Louisville, KY: Westminster John Knox Press, 1996), 3.
[102] Gerstenberger, *Leviticus*, 3.
[103] Gerstenberger, *Leviticus*, 4.

Exegetical Analysis: Deuteronomy 24:14–22

This passage uses repetition to emphasize importance and for ease of remembrance. Some form of *ger* is utilized five times in nine verses. Worth is ascribed to the *ger* and defines them as ones who are seen. Additionally, the literary tool of recollection is utilized here to ascribe worth to the *ger*. Verse 22 calls upon the people to remember their lives as *ger* in Egypt. Israel's experience shapes and provides meaning for *ger* in this emerging world of conquest. This fact will be further referenced in the section concerning reimagining the missional ecclesiology of the Black Church. Just as Yahweh displays His benevolence through Israel by making provision for marginalized people, He wants to do the same through the Black Church in contemporary times.

Exegetical Analysis: Deuteronomy 26:1–15

This pericope begins with Moses's admonition to Israel that, as they enter the land, they are to be mindful of the vulnerable people in their midst. The prosperity of Israel is directly tied to fulfilling Yahweh's command to care for the *ger*. Verse three follows the pattern of remembering in Deuteronomy by referring to the ancestors of the Hebrews. There is a connection between the Hebrew people as *ger* and people who will come into the promised land as *ger* (see verses 5–7, 10–11). As reminders of Yahweh's kindness to them, the text affirms the transition from sojourner to indigenous. The people recount the experience of their ancestor Abram in Egypt. They acknowledge that Yahweh is giving them the land and therefore they will joyfully bring Him the first fruits. Christensen contributes additional insights, stating,

> According to the law of the tithe in 14:22–27, "the tithe of your produce" was presented annually at the central sanctuary,

where it was consumed by the worshipper and his household during the three pilgrimage festivals. At the end of every three years, the tithe was presented in the local towns to provide for [the] needs of the 'Levite,' the 'alien,' the 'orphan,' and the 'widow.'[104]

The protections for the vulnerable became ingrained in the liturgy of Hebrew worship. Central to worship is caring for those who are vulnerable.

Exegetical Analysis: Leviticus 19:9–10; 33–34

Noticeable again in this passage is the pattern of repetition. Erhard Gerstenberger accentuated a striking feature of this text: "God's 'formula of self-introduction,' 'I am Yahweh (your God),' is used more frequently than elsewhere in the Old Testament as an organizational device."[105] This distinction is especially important as the people are living in close proximity to Yahweh. They must be holy as they live and walk with Yahweh. Because Israel is walking closely with God, they must carry His statutes closely to their hearts. Therefore, as Yahweh cares for the *ger*, so must Israel.

Exegetical Analysis: Leviticus 25:35–38

What initially stood out to me in this pericope was how the laws governing the treatment of *ger* provide a baseline for treating other persons who become vulnerable. Gerstenberger points out that verses 35–38 deal with indebtedness. It is essential that Israel keep Yahweh's commands towards the *ger* because members of the land can become the *ger*.

---

[104] Duane L. Christensen, *Christensen World Biblical Commentary: Deuteronomy 21:10–34:12* (Nashville, TN: Thomas Nelson, 2002), 12.
[105] Gerstenberger, *Leviticus*, 261.

Summary of Exegetical Work

Due to the scope of this paper, I could not provide an extensive exegetical analysis of the four passages selected. However, what has been made evident to me through a close reading of the selected texts and exegetical analysis is that there are layers of meaning surrounding the term *ger*. Both the context and experience of those hosting the *ger* contribute to the definition. Furthermore, Old Testament texts demonstrate that Yahweh was extremely mindful of the *ger*. He saw them, He protected them, He provided for them, He embraced them, and He commanded his people to do the same, so much so that part of offering true worship to God is caring for the *ger*. These sentiments are echoed in the New Testament writings of James who states, "Religion that is pure and undefiled before God, the Father, is this: to care for orphans and widows in their distress, and to keep oneself unstained by the world."[106] The meaning of the *ger* must be contextualized to fit the specific circumstances of the land and the *ger* therein. The definition must evolve and expand; however, it should never lose its foundation of love.

A Holistic Definition of Ger

In preparing to identify practical applications for the Black Church to pursue, I find it necessary to review the definitions identified from the analysis of the selected texts: (1) *Ger* is an embraced people according to a broad view of Leviticus. Central to worship in Israel is caring for those who are vulnerable. (2) The *ger*, according to Gerstenberger, were (are) people in danger of losing their economic independence. (3) *Ger* can also be defined as vulnerable people called to be protected by those empowered to do so. (4) *Ger* are people provided for by the community. If I were to preach a sermon in the Black Church tradition, I might use alliteration to identify

---

[106] Jas. 1:27. Unless otherwise noted, all biblical citations are taken from the NRSV.

the four P's of the *ger*. They are promoted in praise, prone to financial pain, protected by God and the Church, and provided for by the community. As stated previously, my personal definition of *ger* acknowledges they are special people who are brought close by Yahweh within a religious congregation. They represent people groups who have been relocated to a place that is unfamiliar, leaving them vulnerable to the power brokers of that place. The Black Church must draw from its reservoir of experience to protect and advocate for the people. Just as the children of Israel came out of slavery and became indigenous in a new land, Black people came to the Americas as slaves and have become in many ways indigenous to and empowered in the Americas. This empowerment must be stewarded well by the Black Church. I propose this is accomplished by reimagining mission, specifically towards the *ger* in her midst, if the Black Church is going to remain viable in the future.

A New Missional Ecclesiology

African Americans connect to the Hebrew narrative of Exodus and living as sojourners. It is now necessary for the Black Church to mine the hidden treasures Yahweh left for the creation of a just society. The Black Church must unlock and apply Yahweh's code of care for the *ger* to cast a prophetic vision for creating justice. Strengthened by the Church's own struggle for equality, the Black Church stands positioned to resist injustice on behalf of others just as it has done for Black people in the past. In the words of Dr. King, "Injustice anywhere is a threat to justice everywhere."[107] The Black Church now stands as a watchman and brother's keeper to modern-day *ger* in her midst.

As noted earlier, trends indicate changing demographics surrounding historically Black churches, causing a slowing of church

---

[107] Martin Luther King, Jr., "Letter From Birmingham Jail," *The Atlantic Monthly* 212, no. 2 (August 1963): 78–88.

growth. Leviticus and Deuteronomy provide a moral, religious, and social justice plan that can mobilize plateaued churches to recapture their action-oriented roots to provide relevant solutions to the *ger* in their midst. Susanna Snyder contributes to the conversation of modern involvement in serving the *ger*: "Opportunities abound in the U.S. to revisit Yahweh's kindness and provision for modern-day *ger*."[108] Like Israel, I believe the U.S. sojourn of the Black Church has uniquely gifted it to minister to the *ger* in its midst.

A good place to start is gaining an understanding of the concept of "sanctuary." Philip Marfleet introduces readers to the concept of providing sanctuary for the vulnerable, the church's historic role of providing sanctuary in Europe, and the abdication of that obligation. He describes the evolution of the current people movement in our world, stating, "by the nineteenth century, with state-centric movements prompting radical change across Europe, sanctuary as an institution guaranteed by the church was at an end."[109] The rise of the nation state threatened and, in many cases, ended the practice of sanctuary. This history is valuable to help Black churches understand the present gap in care added to modern-day *ger* and the opportunities for Black churches to close that gap in care. One final note I found interesting was Marfleet's references to the Underground Railroad as a system of sanctuary in the U.S. The Black Church has a rich legacy to lean on for the purposes of caring for the *ger* in her midst.

Empowering the Marginalized

As this paper begins to shift into practical applications, I want to introduce a few ancient Church disciplines and practices that may assist Black Church leaders in their quest to engage *ger* in their

---

[108] Susanna Snyder, *Asylum-Seeking: Migration and Church* (Burlington, VT: Ashgate Publishing Company, 2012), 4.
[109] Philip Marfleet, "Understanding 'Sanctuary': Faith and Traditions of Asylum," *Journal of Refugee Studies*, 24, no. 3 (July 28, 2011), 449

community. (1) *Lectio Divina*: This contemplative practice of Scripture reading allows readers to meditate on the richness of a text. (2) Listening: This practice of intimacy with God slows believers down and focuses their attention on what God is saying versus what they want to say to God. (3) Lament: This practice can be engaged both individually and corporately. Lament provides space for individuals to communicate their distress and unfavorable emotions towards a circumstance while trusting in God's faithfulness to bring the person through the situation. Corporate lament is often a weapon for oppressed people to use in their fight for equality. Empowered people groups can also use lament to find solidarity with and advocate for those who cannot advocate for themselves. (4) Stewardship: This practice is often associated with money. Stewardship encompasses not only financial management but also managing human resources, facilities, partnerships, skills, privilege, and more in a manner that glorifies God. I suggest that the Black Church steward its rich legacy of empowerment to empower the *ger*. (5) Hospitality: It is the practice of making room for and welcoming those who are outside of one's community. Hospitality is an integral practice that can help Black churches serve the *ger* in their communities. (6) Group Discernment: This is the practice of faith communities seeking God together. It allows people of different backgrounds to humbly join as they seek the Lord for justice and mercy on behalf of the most vulnerable in their midst.

Conclusion

As Eddie Glaude Jr. rightly points out, "the death of the Black church as we have known it occasions an opportunity to breathe new life into what it means to be black and Christian."[110] The Black Church Movement is living in a brave new world. Velli-Mati Kärkkäinen declares

---

[110] Fluker, *Ground Has Shifted*, 9.

that humanity lives in a "diverse and pluralistic world."[111] Globalization, the internet, and massive migration across the globe have all placed the masses, with vastly different beliefs and cultures, in proximity to one another. Additionally, urban forces such as gentrification have reshaped the landscape in which Black churches exist. Greater still is the massive civil rights movement that was sparked by the high visibility of unarmed Black men and women being killed by White police officers.

In its current context, the Black Church Movement has two missional objectives to achieve. First, the Black Church must discern how to address social ills with an eroded testimony and growing religious pluralism. Second, the Black Church must discern how to empower the new marginalized people while continuing to empower the Black community. I argue that for the Black Church Movement to remain viable, the Church must reimagine her missional ecclesiology while holding onto the lessons and legacy imparted by her forebears. Black Church leaders must first locate themselves and their own experiences in the Black Church. They then must recall the legacy of the Black Church while being honest about their current challenges. Next Black Church leaders need to glean from Israel, God's heart for the *ger*, remembering they too were once strangers. Finally, Black Church leaders must reimagine their missional ecclesiology, particularly as it relates to missionally crossing cultural differences to care for the masses who are being displaced around the world and moving into their neighborhoods.

As I conclude, I do so by presenting questions for further research. What work has already been done to empower Black Church leaders to embrace a missional ecclesiology that prioritizes serving the *ger* in their midst? What cultural differences may present roadblocks for the *ger* receiving care from the Black Church? Finally, what narratives

---

[111] Velli-Matti Kärkkäinen, *Hope and Community: A Constructive Christian Theology for the Pluralistic World* (Grand Rapids, MI: William B. Eerdmans Publishing Company, 2017), 1.

must be learned by both the Black Church and the *ger* to see the *ger* truly empowered? The future of the Black Church may currently be in question. These words from a traditional Black Church song provide comfort, hope, and a joyful expectation of what God can and will do through the Black Church serving the *ger* in her midst:

> We've Come This Far By Faith,
>
> Leaning On The Lord.
>
> Trusting In His Holy Word.
>
> He's Never Failed Us Yet.
>
> Oh, Oh- Oh- Can't Turn Around,
>
> We've Come This Far By Faith.[112]

---

[112] Albert A. Goodson, "We've Come This Far By Faith," *Glory To God: The Presbyterian Hymnal* (Louisville, KY: Presbyterian Publishing Corporation, 1956), 656.

Embodied Remembrance: Attachment-Narrative Reflections on the Spiritually Resilient Voice of the Martyrs

Lori E. Banfield

On my first day of classes each semester, as a part of their introduction, I ask students to share a brief story about one of their bodily scars. Typically, I will lead them off by sharing one of my own—the age I was, who I was with, how it all went down, the place we were, and even the scar's position on my body. This moment of reflection allows students to tap into the gift of storytelling that gives their new peers a glimpse into their unique journey, sense of belonging, and, most of all, the gift of God's mercy they represent. Such moments of storytelling become infectious as students, once shy and reserved, begin to vie for the next opportunity to show and tell. Often, these shared moments are filled with laughter, gasps, and empathic reverence for what their neighbor has experienced deep listening and a communal sense of healing becomes evident in the space as an unconscious weaving and bonding through the vulnerable exchange goes forth. In this, I came to realize a meaningful story that might have all been forgotten, if not for the scar on our bodies and the place to honor it.

I call this merciful, meaningful moment, "Sacred Scars." That scar, most often hidden and ignored, is brought out of the shadows of silent suffering to expose God's marvelous light. If, as Rumi posits, "the wound is the place where light enters you,"[113] then, our scars are sacred—embossed with the Spirit of God intimately operating as healer (*Rapha*) and helper (*Ezer*). Scars are a bodily testimony of God's extended mercy toward beloved creation. Though they originated in an experience of harm, they act as a reminder of the resilient purpose and assignment still trusted to our life. Moreover, scars operate as memory markers; they remind us of lessons learned and resilience awakened from pain. They humble us and remind us of our fragility but also our hope of the creator God still at work in us. The story we tell of our scars then invites others into the journey of our healing. The scar is evidence of resilience, but the courage to tell the story—to testify—brings with it the gift of spiritual resilience. Inspired by Romans 5:3–5, spiritual resilience is endurance birthed out of one's sense of their sacred identity cultivated by an active attachment to God (Higher Power); the persistent reliance on one's covenantal faith.[114] Since 2017, a large portion of my research and practice has been centered on conceptualizing and uncovering facets of spiritual resilience, most notably with marginalized people groups in the U.S. like male returning citizens.[115] In 2019, I published research not only establishing spiritual resilience as a working term within the field of psychology, but as a valuable variable within the sustainability of reentry goals and the longevity of healthy habits and connections within African American men transitioning out of incarceration. This research also provided credibility to the essential role faith communities play in the development of spiritual resilience and, thereby, reentry success. Returning

---

[113] Linda LeBoutillier, "The Wound Is the Place Where the Light Enters," *Reaching for The Sky* (blog), February 13, 2014, https://mettahu.wordpress.com/2014/02/13/the-wound-is-the-place-where-the-light-enters/.

[114] Lori E. Banfield, "Fostering Spiritual Resilience and Vitality in Formerly Incarcerated Persons of African American Descent," *Journal of Pastoral Care & Counseling* 73, no. 4 (2019): 223.

[115] "Returning citizens" is a dignifying characterization of individuals transitioning out of the system of incarceration back into civil society.

citizens, mostly males of melanated glory, have endured multiple wounds and scarring within this society. Granting secure space to testify to such scars has been one of four enhancers of spiritual resilience I have deduced within Black life.[116]

Given my fascination with testimony, I have become increasingly intrigued by the transcendent voice—those not only absent from our purview but those absent from the body as well as the voice of creation as expressed in Psalm 19:1–4. In reading Psalm 19 not simply as an anthropomorphic metaphor but giving it literal consideration, I position myself to ask: if I am designed in connection with this creation, how will I allow their echoes of testimony to influence the story I tell?

Attachment-narrative reflections on the voice of the martyrs, including that of land that has been desecrated, remind us that our witness has both eternal implications and eternal longevity, impacting and influencing generations beyond our purview. Matthew 10:28 reminds us, "Don't be afraid of those who want to kill your body; they cannot touch your soul."[117] Testimony or witness can never die; the soundwaves of our soul continue to echo and reverberate off the ways of creation—because the Word of God cannot return void. Testimony resounds, and the scars, uncovered and unmuted, sing a song the angels cannot sing. A people of community and oral tradition, historically disenfranchised and deprived of objective provisions of value on this soil, we—the collaboration of the Indigenous and African descendants—have brilliantly honored one another with the inheritance of priceless verbal wisdom, complex artistry, and fortuitous ritual tradition. Hence, it behooves us to embrace silent and embodied remembrance of even our scarred places in history

---

[116] I acknowledge four enhancers of spiritual resilience, especially valuable for people of melanated glory: Social Capital (Community), Ritual (and ceremonial rites of passage), Place, and Testimony.

[117] Unless otherwise noted, all biblical citations are taken from the New Living Translation.

that pressed out such rich oil. Such embrace intently attunes to the echoes of person, and place (sacred space) so we might reckon what was and envision what can be.

Take a moment and consider one of your own sacred scars: where were you, what happened, who was there, who cared for you or participated in your restoration? As you indulge this flashbulb memory in your mind, can you also begin to feel the physical and emotional harm again faintly? As you listen intently to your body's story, let us consider it in the context of the Apostle Paul's words in Romans 8:16–25:

> For his Spirit joins with our spirit to affirm that we are God's children. And since we are his children, we are his heirs. In fact, together with Christ we are heirs of God's glory. But if we are to share his glory, we must also share his suffering. Yet what we suffer now is nothing compared to the glory he will reveal to us later. For all creation is waiting eagerly for that future day when God will reveal who his children really are. Against its will, all creation was subjected to God's curse. But with eager hope, the creation looks forward to the day when it will join God's children in glorious freedom from death and decay. For we know that all creation has been groaning as in the pains of childbirth right up to the present time. And we believers also groan, even though we have the Holy Spirit within us as a foretaste of future glory, for we long for our bodies to be released from sin and suffering. We, too, wait with eager hope for the day when God will give us our full rights as his adopted children, including the new bodies he has promised us. We were given this hope when we were saved.

Considering this passage and using a psychological and biblical attachment-narrative framework, I call into consideration the echoing witness of creation. This witness is perceived through the groaning witness of persons, places, and punctures (blemishes) absent from our purview. Experiences of embodied remembrance via active listening to the transcendent testimony of the martyred beloved and the desecrated land as the sacred scars of this life can enhance personal spiritual resilience and communal efforts of dignity restoration and reconciliation.

As an attachment-narrative clinician holding a Gospelist lens, I have become increasingly sensitive to the formative and restorative power of remembrance in sound/word and motion/deed among our people of melanated glory. An attachment-narrative approach is a fusion of attachment theory's premise and narrative therapy's techniques. Both are psychological in discipline but provide insights into our biblical and theological commitments. Attachment theory posits that humans are relational beings whose bonds or attachments (felt, perceived, and, I would add, desired) play a foundational, formative role in the development of a person, including their physical, socio-emotional, and identity development as well as their cognitive capacity to envision.[118] Such bonds firstly begin with persons (subjective), but quickly are shared with objects, places (e.g., a home) and things (e.g., toys). And then, as we engage, our imagination takes on a transcendent quality wherein we express emotional bonds with people, places, and things outside our purview (e.g., imaginary friends in childhood, God, and even those deceased).

Narrative therapy's techniques of storytelling and testimony provide a liberating experience of healing through recalling and reimagining experiences in one's life. At its foundation, narrative theory takes a communal approach to valuing an individual's story and aims to empower them as both storytellers and encourage their proactive, hopeful prose.[119] Together, attachment-narrative provides a framework

---

[118] David G. Myers, and C. N. DeWall, *Psychology in Modules*, 13th ed. (New York: Worth, 2021), 180–185.
[119] Edward P. Wimberly, *Counseling African American Marriages and Families* (Louisville, KY: Westminster John Knox Press, 1997), 2–6.

for us to view how attachment bonds—perceived and felt, desired and denied, present and transcendent, subjective and objective—have the power to influence our personal story.[120] As such, we become aware of the ways we view ourselves, the world, and the place we operate in, as well as our capacity to envision a future self in relation to our thematic reality. Even more so for collectivist people groups (i.e., Afro-Asiatic, Caribbean, Greek, Latinx, etc.), the capacity to thrive and the potential trajectory of one's story is heavily intertwined with the level of relational bonds one acknowledges and embodies. Embodiment occurs through memory, ritual activity, place visitation, and a variety of honored or customed sounds and gestures.

My current inquisition centers on bonds that are ruptured, or scars of suffering inflicted upon persons and places—what Paul identifies in verse 20 as an undesired subjugation to God's curse. Per verses 21 and 23, we can deduce God's curse as "death and decay . . . sin and suffering" that results in our groanings of lament. I wrestle with the history of genocidal activity perpetuated against my people of the African diaspora and Indigenous to North American soil. I ponder how we as their lineage are to respond to the reality of broken trust and the selfish desecration of body and land because of one's melanated image and their witness to the image they bare.

The passage in Romans draws attention to the reality of these relational rupture sufferings as a collective subjection to God's curse but then affirms its temporality because of the redemptive reconciliation of Christ's salvific work. Jesus's suffering was a semicolon, not a period in the story of glory. Thus, we have inherited through our redeemed—or restored—attachment bond with God the Father. With that same posture, we can now "with eager hope . . . [look] forward to the day when [we] will join God's children in glorious freedom from

---

[120] Rudi Dallos, *Attachment Narrative Therapy: Integrating Systemic, Narrative and Attachment Approaches* (London: Open University Press, 2006). 1–3.

death and decay."[121] We can see then how our attachments are shaping our identity and, thereby, our view and pursuit of what can be.

I'd also like to turn our attention to the moments in between suffering and glory. Though suffering does not last, scars can linger and, with them, the echo of our response. Paul writes, "all creation has been groaning as in pains of childbirth . . . and we believers also groan."[122] When ruptures or breaks in bonds occur, our person (body, mind, and soul) is compelled to respond. Our soul responds in lament. Our mind responds in meaning-making and evaluation of the suffering's intensity and impact, as well as attempts to problem-solve. Our body responds with somatic stimulation and emotional acknowledgment of the loss, also known as grief. Paul aptly summarizes this holistic experience of grief response as groaning. As an extension of my thesis, I posit that groaning is a valuable voice in the narrative of our redemption and reconciliation. The Holy Spirit even makes intercession on humanity's behalf with groanings.[123] Thus, acknowledgement, listening, and remembrance of the place (time and space) of groanings becomes advantageous to our actualized experience of restoration and reconciliation.

Acknowledgment, listening, and remembrance are core features of the attachment-narrative therapeutic process and approach I employ. To provide a restorative balm, one must listen well to the place of suffering. This is no different than how we ought to engage the lingering scars of our day. In 2022, I was able to return to Israel to explore, in place, the sacred scars of our Judeo-Christian faith, ancient Afro-Asiatic ancestors, and the European Jewish community. Yad Vashem, The World Holocaust Remembrance Center, is a space constructed with great intention from its architecture, landscape, and standards to honor and walk in embodied remembrance of those six million image bearers martyred during the German state-sanctioned genocidal strategy

---

[121] Rom. 8:20–21.
[122] Rom. 8:22–23.
[123] Rom. 8:26.

of the Nazi regime from 1933–1945.[124] A 4,200 square-meter site in Jerusalem, Yad Vashem is constructed upon a mountain with its main features structured in the shape of a triangular spike cutting through and protruding out of the mountain peak to a gorgeously expansive landscape. Its layout is designed to guide participants in the zigzag maze of evils-consuming progression. Patrons are charged to trek through in complete silence so they might look, feel, and, most of all, listen to the voices, as if to say, admonished in the spirit of Genesis 4:10, listen, your brother and sister's blood and breath cry out from the ground.

As I walked through the personal artifacts, images, and audio recordings of persons martyred and those who survived, I began to experience a nearness and, thereby, a righteous indignation to lament and actively pursue dignifying justice. An encounter that is vividly imprinted on my mind and heart is a wagon full of shoes. These were a collection of the actual shoes of those who had been led to the gas chambers. Shoes of all sizes. I sat with them and listened to their footsteps—I pondered where they had gone the days before and where they could have gone. The shoes became, for me, another direct symbol of the scar and groaning. As I looked them over, my eyes caught a glimpse of a shoe that appeared to be the same size as my five-year-old daughter. I was compelled to consider the story my own daughter's shoes tell and all the hopes I have for her feet to grow and pursue the peace and justice of Kingdom Come. Moreover, I considered the ways I and her father worked at protecting and supporting that pursuit. For the second time in three years, I left Yad Vashem with a deep gratitude and capacity to envision that felt guided by the Spirit through listening to the transcendent testimony—the voice and groanings of those martyred.

---

[124] "The Holocaust History Museum," Yad Vashem: The World Holocaust Remembrance Center, accessed December 1, 2023, https://www.yadvashem.org/museum/holocaust-history-museum.html.

I began to think of the spaces in which we, as people of the African diaspora and Indigenous descent, honor the martyrs of our ancestry. I am grateful that in recent American years we have witnessed the investment and opening of sacred spaces of remembrance like the National Museum of African American History and Culture (Washington, DC). Another museum that is akin to Yad Vashem is the National Memorial for Peace and Justice, also known as the Lynching Museum, curated by Bryan Stevenson and the Equal Justice Initiative in Montgomery, Alabama. Here we can practice embodied remembrance in recognition of the scars of racial terror coming out of the shadows and in honor of God's glory resiliently revealed in the personhood of our ancestors. Spaces (places and times) to remember and feel the scar again, to acknowledge its existence, consider its meaning and its impact, and honor its voice to become a restorative agent in the mission of Kingdom Come. If we are to present the Kingdom of Heaven in the earth authentically, then the martyr's voice and groans cannot be undervalued or overlooked, for they have a valued place in the dialogue of Heaven.[125]

As a diasporic people disproportionately familiar with strife, struggle, and suffering, Black Christians have been a steadfast example (living monument) to the restorative, sustaining power of embodied remembrance in person and place. Through time, we have expressed a variety of mourning rituals and celebration of life traditions to mark time and acknowledge the tension of hope-laden scars. No doubt this way of living and honor is also affirmed in the Holy Scriptures through the people of God, elect and grafted in. The people of God

---

[125] Rev. 6:9–11: "When the Lamb broke the fifth seal, I saw under the altar the souls of all who had been martyred for the word of God and for being faithful in their testimony. They shouted to the Lord and said, 'O Sovereign Lord, holy and true, how long before you judge the people who belong to this world and avenge our blood for what they have done to us?' Then a white robe was given to each of them. And they were told to rest a little longer until the full number of their brothers and sisters—their fellow servants of Jesus who were to be martyred—had joined them."

move through life making the intergenerational exchanges of identity, wisdom, and wealth through practices of embodied remembrance and honoring of those who have gone on.

In conclusion, I offer for contrast our consideration of Romans 8:16–25 with the later promise expressed in Isaiah 55:12–13 (ESV):

> For you shall go out in joy and be led forth in peace; the mountains and the hills before you shall break forth into singing, and all the trees of the field shall clap their hands. Instead of the thorn shall come up the cypress; instead of the brier shall come up the myrtle; and it shall make a name for the Lord, an everlasting sign that shall not be cut off.

Here Isaiah depicts the future glory of restoration for God's creation. He describes the earth's joyful, restorative response to humanity's acceptance of God's trustworthy salvation. Here, God testifies of God's self. He distinguishes himself from the unreliable sayings of humanity. God simply conveys that there is no need for his beloved people to feel insecure or jaded by hope when he speaks because it has no choice but to spring forth out of whatever position it was in. This passage is also important as it is the inspiration text for the exit moment of Yad Vashem—the National Holocaust Museum. Upon leaving the room of silent tears walled with photos of martyrs, patrons are led straight ahead up a small incline outward to this view. The walk takes visitors from suffering to scar, groaning to glory. Memorials like Yad Vashem and the National Memorial for Peace and Justice are a critical model in the healing balm and fruit of leaning into the martyred witness. As we consider the outlook when exiting Yad Vashem, we get a view of the new horizon, an overlook upon the sacred land, promise and responsibility of Kingdom Come.

I wonder, what do you see when you look out on the places you and your ancestors inhabit? How does the land's testimony of rupture and renewal evoke you to see as a possibility for the people?

One of the things that separates humans from other creatures is our ability to envision ourselves in the future (based on where we have been or what we have already experienced)—to anticipate experience and thereby even embody that experience before it happens (anticipatory grief, joy, angst). This, then, can dictate how we move forward and our decisions. The anticipatory envisioning is in large part due to our complex memory capacity and relational posture. Memories are stored and processed in two major areas of our brain (the hippocampus and the cortex). The hippocampus is where all our experiences are initially processed, and if they have an emotional connection or a meaningful attachment, they will become inextricably linked to those areas of our body and the position in space (or place) that responded with emotion to the initial intense occurrence or reoccurring experiences. Our brains actively associate place or space with experience and allow our meaningful (emotionally/heart-charged) memories to mold our strategies for what is to come. Through neuroplasticity, we are forming new neural pathways, new neural attachment bonds that dictate our anticipatory engagements and cognitive processing.

The act of remembrance that leads to forward-thinking is an essential thread within the tapestry of Scripture. Remembrance exposes our valued connections or bonds and, thereby, our anchors of resilience and posture toward promise. As people of melanated glory, we descend from those who intentionally showed their value of place and space, person and purpose, through ritual, rites of passage, testimony, art, and other gestures of embodied remembrance. So, Jesus' edict to "do this in remembrance of me!"[126] hits differently in its intention of embodiment and formation. Consideration of the scars among us and upon us can reveal the beauty of God's redeeming glory at work in us "giving you the desire and the power to do what pleases him."[127]

---

[126] Luke 22:18–20; 1 Cor. 11:23–25.
[127] Phil. 2:13.

Progressing Together: A Gospelist Approach on Addressing Racial Discrimination within the Workplace

Charonda Woods-Boone

Introduction

The Lord values work because He created it. God worked when He created the heavens and the earth and everything in them. In Genesis 2:15, God placed Adam in the Garden to tend over it and Adam was instructed to work and maintain it. In Christ's love, humility, and humanity, He not only laid His life down for the sins of the world, but He also worked as a carpenter.[128] *The Apostle Paul worked to make a living as a tentmaker, and he used this work as a bridge for ministry.*[129] *Scripture attests that vocational work is a form of worship unto God.*[130] *Yet, it is hard to work diligently unto the Lord when people and systems prevent individuals from flourishing in their work.*

The United States of America was built on racial discrimination as European settlers enslaved Africans and forced them to build this country's infrastructure and economy through agricultural labor.

---

[128] Mark 6:3. Unless otherwise noted, all biblical citations are taken from the New International Version.
[129] Acts 18.
[130] Col. 3:23–24.

After the abolition of slavery, racism persisted in various areas of African American life. One area in which racial discrimination pervades numerous African American lives is the workplace.[131] *The workplace is central for many African Americans as roughly twenty-one million African Americans work today.*[132] After more than five decades of federal legislation in the United States designed to protect workers against discrimination (Title VII of the Civil Rights Act of 1964), workplace racial discrimination remains a prevalent issue for African Americans. For the purposes of this research, I define workplace racial discrimination as unfair conditions, dismissiveness, reduced opportunities, or negative treatment based on an employee's African ancestry.

Common results of this unfair treatment in the workplace include Black Americans facing the highest unemployment rate of any racial or ethnic group in the country,[133] poorer employee benefits, fewer promotional opportunities, and greater risk of job instability.[134] Additionally, Black American workers report heightened stress levels and pressure to outperform their White peers, and they have been manipulated to fulfill additional roles and work responsibilities. These are often roles that they were neither hired to perform nor compensated to complete.[135] Workplace racial discrimination has socioeconomic, physiological, and psychological impacts. I posit that racial inequality within the workplace is an injustice and must cease because God values work and justice for all His creation. *A Gospelist view, or* **Gospel**

---

[131] Throughout this paper, I will use African Americans and Black Americans interchangeably and these represent North Americans that have African Ancestry.

[132] "Labor Force Statistics from the Current Population Survey," U.S. Bureau of Labor Statistics, accessed March 3, 2024, https://www.bls.gov/cps/cpsaat03.htm.

[133] "Labor Force Statistics," accessed October 9, 2023.

[134] Christian E. Weller, "African Americans Face Systemic Obstacles to Getting Good Jobs," *The Center for American Progress*, accessed October 3, 2023, https://www.americanprogress.org/article/african-americans-face-systematic-obstacles-getting-good-jobs/.

[135] Gillian B. White, "Black Workers Really Do Need to Be Twice as Good," *The Atlantic*, October 7, 2015, https://www.theatlantic.com/business/archive/2015/10/why-black-workers-really-do-need-to-be-twice-as-good/409276/.

Haymanot, *insists upon a biblical, Gospel-centric approach to any injustice.*[136] *Such ideals affirm that the way to expel injustice is for believers to progress together and unite in this fight.* The Apostle Paul writes in Ephesians 2:10, "For you are God's handiwork, created in Christ Jesus to do *good works*, which God prepared in advance for us to do."[137] For Christians, Ephesians 2:10 is an anchored text for this Gospel-centric justice work within the workplace. Therefore, the goal of this paper is to call believers to collective action to address racial discrimination within the workplace. Additionally, this paper will contain historical, communal ways African Americans have confronted workplace racial discrimination and provide a practical theology for Christians to address workplace racial discrimination in light of Gospel Haymanot.

Evidence of Workplace Racial Discrimination

Often when I have dinner with African American friends who work in different industries such as academia, medicine, and government, we find ourselves venting to one another about the many ways we have been ignored or mistreated at work. I used to wonder if this was only happening to me and my local friend group—until I began to research. I found out that in a February 2023 study, 41 percent of Black workers said that they have been discriminated against or have been treated unfairly by an employer in hiring, pay, and promotions,

---

[136] Vince L. Bantu, ed., *Gospel Haymanot: A Constructive Theology and Critical Reflection on African and Diasporic Christianity* (Calumet City, IL: UMI, 2020), 8–9. *Haymanot* is a Ge'ez word (language from ancient Ethiopia) that means "belief," "faith," or "theology." In the face of the Transatlantic Slave Trade, traditionally African Americans have stood on Gospel Haymanot which affirms the authority of Scripture and justice for all. Biblical orthodoxy and justice for all are inseparable. Racial discrimination within the workplace is an injustice and it declares spiritual, physical, and social liberation be in place for all.
[137] Emphasis added.

due to their ethnicity.[138] Moreover, Black Americans over the age of forty-seven reported a 60 percent higher rate of discrimination than Whites.[139] In a 2022 Pew Research Study, it was reported that Black American workers earn less than U.S. workers overall. Regarding full-time wage and salary workers, the median weekly earnings for Black American workers ages sixteen and older are $878, compared with $1,059 for all U.S. workers in the same age group. Additionally, when looking at performance evaluations, 56 percent of Black Americans say that racial and ethnic bias is a major issue.[140] The other ways in which Black Americans are discriminated against in the workplace are upsetting. More than 66 percent of women of color in a *Harvard Business Review* survey shared that they have been mistaken for admins or custodial staff at work.[141] Black Americans are most likely to say that they have been discriminated against more than any other race or ethnicity.[142] Among Black American workers, 51 percent say that being Black makes it harder to succeed where they work.[143] While casually venting to one another about racial discrimination may relieve some stress, we must take action to address the offenders, to fulfill our

---

[138] Katherine Schaeffer, "Black Workers' Views and Experiences in the U.S. Labor Force Stand out in Key Ways," accessed September 30, 2023, https://www.pewresearch.org/short-reads/2023/08/31/black-workers-views-and-experiences-in-the-us-labor-force-stand-out-in-key-ways/.

[139] Desta Fekedulegn et al., "Prevalence of Workplace Discrimination and Mistreatment in a National Sample of Older U.S. Workers: The REGARDS Cohort Study," *SSM-Population Health*, vol. 8 (2019), https://www.sciencedirect.com/science/article/pii/S2352827319300588?via%3Dihub.

[140] Schaeffer, "Black Workers' Views."

[141] Joan C. Williams, Olivia Andrews, and Mikayla Boginsky, "Why Many Women of Color Don't Want to Return to the Office," *Harvard Business Review*, May 12, 2022, https://hbr.org/2022/05/why-many-women-of-color-dont-want-to-return-to-the-office. Web 29 September 2023.

[142] Juliana Menasce Horowitz and Kim Parker, "How Americans View Their Jobs," Pew Research Center, March 30, 2023, https://www.pewresearch.org/social-trends/2023/03/30/how-americans-view-their-jobs/.

[143] Schaeffer, "Black Workers' Views."

Ephesians 2:10 biblical mandate, and to address the socioeconomic, *physiological*, and psychological damage wrought by discrimination.

The Biblical, Socioeconomic, Physiological, and Psychological Significance of Progressing Together

Our work matters to God both now and eternally. Pierre Martinot-Lagarde proposes that because Christ is "the measure, model, and horizon of Christian life,"[144] Christians should seek to promote a sustainable institutional and economic labor environment. Christians should also develop and enhance measures of social-labor protection, encourage social dialogue, demonstrate respect, and enable the realization of fundamental principles and rights at work.[145] Racial discrimination is an injustice that concerns God. Progressing together to eradicate workplace racial discrimination has biblical, socioeconomic, physiological, and psychological significance. Biblically speaking, Scripture instructs believers to live a godly witness based on our profession of faith.[146] Believers are representatives of Jesus Christ wherever they go, and this includes the workplace; believers should implore others in speech and *action* to come to God the Father through Jesus Christ.[147]

> More specifically, believers should walk in the godly, communicable attribute of justice because we serve a just God.[148] Gospel Haymanot demands justice in every form.

---

[144] Pierre Martinot-Lagarde, "Theology of Work, Opportunities and Challenges," *Dignity of Work: Theological and Interdisciplinary Perspectives*, ed. Kenneth Mtata (Geneva, Switzerland: Lutheran University Press, 2011), 72.
[145] Kenneth Mtata, ed., *Dignity of Work: Theological and Interdisciplinary Perspectives* (Minneapolis, MN: Lutheran University Press, 2011), 72.
[146] Col. 3:23.
[147] 2 Cor. 5:20.
[148] Eccles. 3:17; Mic. 6:8; Heb. 10:30.

Addressing racial inequality and injustice on your job, is you standing up for the current and next generation because you believe God's beloved deserve to be treated with equality and respect. Taking up the mantle to battle workplace racial discrimination is a Gospel witness that embodies Christ's heart for humanity. Joseph exhibited a godly witness while being unjustly imprisoned for a crime he did not commit. While in prison, he still allowed God to use him as he interpreted the dreams of the cupbearer and baker of the king of Egypt.[149] Although everyone's fight is not yours, your participation in vocalizing injustice on your job is a demonstration of your active faith that you serve a living God who sees and values all.

Progressing together to eradicate workplace racial discrimination has socioeconomic significance. It is the difference between a single African American male having money left over from his paycheck to take a yearly vacation or a Black family being afforded the opportunity to send their child to college. Jonathan Welburn, an expert in economic analysis and the lead author of the wealth gap study, "Overcoming Compound Racial Inequality," said, "Yesterday's segregation is today's wealth gap. We like to pretend that we live in a race-neutral, merit-based society now, that this is all in the past, but you can't erase history. It shows up in our wealth. For many, it shows up in the lack of wealth."[150] Earnings affect wealth. The U.S. Census reports that the racial wealth gap of yesterday and today changes the game for racial

---

[149] Gen. 39–40.
[150] Jonathan W. Welburn et al., "Overcoming Compound Racial Inequity: Policies and Costs for Closing the Black-White Wealth Gap," *Racial Wealth Gap Discussion Paper Series*, December 7, 2022, https://www.rand.org/pubs/research_reports/RRA1259-2.html.

origins, as White householders hold a median household wealth of $187,300 while Black householders only hold $14,100.[151]

The absence of working together to eliminate racial discrimination in the workplace has *physiological* and psychological significance. Racial discrimination has been shown to increase inflammation in the body and decrease cognitive reasoning, thinking, and memory functions.[152] In a 2022 biological psychiatric study, it was shown that discrimination is associated with anxiety, depression, altered self-perception, and a slew of other biological and psychological symptoms that follow behind.[153] Our mental and physical health is on the line. We should seek wellness for our communities and ourselves to continue to live the life God has called us to live, in the workplace. A Christian's biblical mandate and communal African American history inform a practical theology on progressing together to address workplace racial discrimination.

A Practical Theology on Addressing Workplace Racial Discrimination

Believers should understand that our faith in the Lord is foundational to the victories and progress we as African Americans have experienced within the workplace. The following practical theology bears in

---

[151] Neil Bennett, Donald Hays, and Briana Sullivan, "2019 Data Show Baby Boomers Nearly 9 Times Wealthier Than Millennials," United States Census Bureau, August 1, 2022, https://www.census.gov/library/stories/2022/08/wealth-inequality-by-household-type.html.

[152] Joceyln Apodaca Schlossberg, "How Does Racism Make You Sick?" *UCLA Health*, October 24, 2022, https://www.uclahealth.org/news/how-does-racism-make-you-sick.

[153] T. S. Dong et al., "How Discrimination Gets Under the Skin: Biological Determinants of Discrimination Associated with Dysregulation of the Brain-Gut Microbiome System and Psychological Symptoms." *Biological Psychiatry* 94, no. 3 (2023): 203–14, https://www.biologicalpsychiatryjournal.com/article/S0006-3223(22)01703-6/fulltext.

mind a Gospel Haymanot approach to address workplace racial discrimination as it is seen throughout African American history: that there is strength and progress in uniting.

1. *Understand that God sees and values you and others.* To see yourself and others as worthy of this Gospel Haymanot work, you should understand that you and others are God's good creation and God values His creation and the flourishing of their work.[154] God knows what others are intentionally or unintentionally doing to you and others. Exodus 3:7 says, "The Lord said, 'I have surely seen the affliction of My people who are in Egypt, and have given heed to their cry because of their taskmasters, for I am aware of their sufferings.'"[155] God had a plan for the children of Israel in Exodus, and He has a plan for you. Know that the Lord wants to see you thrive in your work and gifts, as we see Psalm 33:5: it is God's agenda to foster equity and justice for all of humanity. In your fight for workplace equality, remember that the Lord is with you. Just like God providentially raised up Joseph during his sexual harassment case with Potiphar's wife,[156] God is joining you in the work of addressing injustices because He has a heart for justice.

2. *Express your concerns.*
    a. *To God.* Express your concerns communally to God in prayer, remembering the cry of Asaph in Psalm 73:1–28. Even though it seems as if the wicked are advancing, God will not let the wicked escape his judgment. Coming together to collectively pray for our enemies within the workplace is biblically mandated.[157] Make the sovereign

---
[154] Gen. 1:26–28, 31.
[155] Exod. 3:7, NASB.
[156] Gen. 39.
[157] Matt. 5:44.

Lord your refuge and seek specific guidance from him in prayer concerning your workplace racial discrimination. The subsequent communal guidance on addressing racial discrimination within your workplace should all be submitted to God in prayer, as our specific plans should be committed to him.[158]

b. *To your community.* Express your concerns to your church family and support groups. Do not suffer alone and in silence. God can work through multiple relationships and networks. Pursue relationships with other believers for support and accountability purposes. Network with other practitioners like yourself, and talk to fellow engineers, professors, and managers as you walk through discrimination at work. Discuss your wages with non-Black American workers—this is your right as an employee.[159] If your workplace does not already have Employee Resource Groups (ERGs) then start one.[160] ERGs can provide opportunities for yourself and others to come together to discuss equitable items to raise to your leadership.

3. *Unite & Unionize.* Unite and unionize to build an alliance for equal opportunities for all. Throughout African American history, using collective power to bargain for better conditions has worked. In 1925, Asa Phillip Randolph met with porters from the Chicago-based Pullman Palace Car Company. The mostly Black Pullman workforce was paid lower wages than White railway workers and faced harsh conditions and long working hours. Over the next ten years, Randolph worked with these

---

[158] Prov. 16:3.
[159] "Your Rights," National Labor Relations Board, accessed May 23, 2023, https://www.nlrb.gov/about-nlrb/rights-we-protect/your-rights.
[160] "What Are Employee Resource Groups?" *U.S. News & World Report*, June 5, 2023, https://money.usnews.com/careers/company-culture/articles/what-are-employee-resource-groups.

workers to form and organize the Brotherhood of Sleeping Car Porters (BSCP) in 1925.[161] The BSCP organized Black porters and maids at the Chicago-based Pullman company, the largest employer of Black workers in the nation. When the union was finally recognized in 1937, it became one of the first predominately Black labor unions in the nation that set the stage for the abolishment of the Jim Crow System. Randolph was also one of the first two Black vice presidents of the American Federation of Labor-Congress of Industrial Organizations (AFL-CIO), and he was the founder of the Negro American Labor Council. These labor organizations were vehicles for Black American advancement, and they gave rise to protest politics in the country. In the 1930s, Secretary of the National Association for the Advancement of Colored People (NAACP), Walter White, Norman Thomas, and A. Phillip Randolph were able to directly alleviate some of the oppressive living and working conditions of its members. This occurred through the strategic use of strikes and public demonstrations under the leadership of Harry L. Mitchell and the Southern Tenant Farmers Union (STFU).[162]

Additional unionized victories include Lucy Parsons in 1886 founding the International Garment Workers Union as she led over 80,000 people to strike in support of the eight-hour workday.[163] Hattie Canty was active in her union, was elected to the executive board of the Culinary Workers Union (CWU) in 1984, and became union president in 1990. She was the first Black woman and the first room attendant elected to this

---

[161] Andrew E. Kersten and Clarence Lang, *Reframing Randolph: Labor, Black Freedom, and the Legacies of A. Philip Randolph* (New York: NYU Press, 2015), 21.
[162] James Gilbert Cassedy, "African Americans and the American Labor Movement. National Archives," *Prologue Magazine* 29, no. 2 (1997), https://www.archives.gov/publications/prologue/1997/summer/american-labor-movement.html#note1.
[163] "Black Women Built That: Labor and Workers' Rights," National Women's Law Center, February 28, 2018, https://nwlc.org/black-women-built-that-labor-and-workers-rights/.

position in CWU. During her tenure, Canty galvanized workers from eighty-four nations, helped push forward racial justice within the industry and her union, and founded the Culinary Training Academy, which helps people of color obtain better jobs in the hospitality industry. In addition, Canty served as president of the CWU during the longest strike in U.S. labor history, leading the workers at the Frontier Hotel through six and a half years of negotiations for better labor standards.[164]

Unions help shrink racial wage gaps. Black American workers who join unions are more likely to receive a bigger wage boost.[165] Unions better socioeconomic status and increase wealth for Black American households, as it was found that Black American households with a union member have median wealth that is more than three times the median wealth of nonunion Black American households.[166] Black American workers are more likely than White American workers to be covered by collective bargaining, and the wage boost they get from being covered by collective bargaining is 13.1%, above the 10.2% average wage boost for unionized workers overall.[167] "Two are better than one, because they have a good return for their labor," says Solomon in Ecclesiastes 4:9, and historically we see from the African American struggle that

---

[164] "5 Black Leaders That Shaped the Labor Movement," National Education Association, January 26, 2023, https://www.nea.org/professional-excellence/student-engagement/tools-tips/5-black-leaders-shaped-labor-movement#:~:text=Over%20the%20next%20ten%20years,labor%20union%20in%20the%20nation.

[165] Elise Gould, "Black-White Wage Gaps Are Worse Today Than in 2000," *Working Economics Blog*, February 27, 2020, https://www.epi.org/blog/black-white-wage-gaps-are-worse-today-than-in-2000/.

[166] Aurelia Glass, David Madland, and Christian E. Weller, "Unions Help Increase Wealth for All and Close Racial Wealth Gaps," The Center for American Progress, September 6, 2021, https://www.americanprogress.org/article/unions-help-increase-wealth-close-racial-wealth-gaps/.

[167] "Unions Help Reduce Disparities and Strengthen Our Democracy," Economic Policy Institute, April 23, 2021, https://www.epi.org/publication/unions-help-reduce-disparities-and-strengthen-our-democracy/.

there is power in numbers. Collectively document racial discrimination workplace facts, then communally work together to demand improved working conditions.

4. *Read your workplace policies and propose changes.* Familiarize yourself with your organization's workplace policies and collectively suggest adding policies where you see gaps. If it is not evident, ask your HR department what their anti-discrimination policy is. Requests from your employer should be made in oral and written form in a conciliatory manner. For apparent wage discrimination, with others, request from your employer summary results from their pay audits. If your employer is not conducting pay audits, then request them. Remind your employer that the U.S. Department of Labor (DOL) can audit employers at any time, and the DOL has historically found wage violations. Ask your company what their goals for representation in their recruitment strategy are. There tends to be less racial discrimination in workplaces where there are more persons of color.[168] You and your ERG should obtain training on Equal Employment Opportunity (EEO) principles and learn about your legal rights and responsibilities under the anti-discrimination laws and ensure your company is following suit.

Additional communal responses for believers include spurring your church and vocational support groups to write your congressperson(s) or elected representatives about the issues individuals face concerning workplace racial discrimination.[169] Progressing together includes believers

---

[168] Becky Strauss, "Battling Racial Discrimination in the Workplace," D.C. Policy Center, January 24, 2019, https://www.dcpolicycenter.org/publications/battling-racial-discrimination-in-the-workplace/.

[169] "Find Your Representative," Unites States House of Representatives, accessed September 4, 2023, https://www.house.gov/representatives/find-your-representative. Use this website to input your ZIP code to vocalize workplace racial discrimination policy solutions.

collectively proposing policies to eliminate and mitigate workplace racial discrimination.

Workplace policy changes can happen when you let your voice be heard through protests. Throughout history, thousands of African Americans have participated in nonviolent protests, sit-ins, and the March on Washington, and they *demanded* equal rights under the law that eventually made Title VII of the Civil Rights Act of 1964 come into effect. Leaders of the Civil Rights era achieved progress for Black American workers. In the example of the Reverend Dr. Martin Luther King's "Letter from Birmingham Jail," this was a win for workplace racial discrimination as it fueled a generational strategy on how to address racial discrimination in a nonviolent manner.[170] This strategy, put forth by Dr. King and others who fought for justice in the Civil Rights era, eventually gave way to desegregation in Birmingham, Alabama, and improved employment programs for Black American workers.[171]

5. *File a discrimination complaint.* If your company is not addressing your collective concerns, then in unison take prompt action and file formal complaints. Internal complaints should be filed first before you file anything with the U.S. Equal Employment Opportunity Commission (EEOC). Document your shared correspondence with your employer(s) about the racial discrimination you are experiencing and, depending on how they respond, remind your employer that retaliation is illegal.[172] If your company retaliates (e.g., disciplinary action,

---

[170] Martin Luther King, Jr. "A Letter from Birmingham Jail," *Ebony* (August, 1963): 23–32.
[171] "Birmingham Campaign," The Martin Luther King Jr. Research and Education Institute, Stanford University, accessed October 13, 2023, https://kinginstitute.stanford.edu/birmingham-campaign.
[172] "What Is Retaliation and How Can I Prevent It?" U.S. Equal Employment Opportunity Commission, accessed October 3, 2023, https://www.eeoc.gov/employers/small-business/8-what-retaliation-and-how-can-i-prevent-it.

demotion, firing) then file a retaliation complaint and submit your documented proof.[173]

If your company dismisses your racial discrimination claim, then file a charge of discrimination with the EEOC.[174] Although many EEOC cases are overlooked or take a very long time to attend to, persist and make your voice heard. Cases are only won if they are filed. There are some successful EEOC-settled cases for African Americans as we see in the following examples. In 2022, Jackson National Life Insurance Co. agreed to pay $20.5 million to settle claims that it discriminated against Black female employees who were paid less than their White colleagues and were passed over for promotion in favor of less-qualified White males. The company allegedly also tolerated a hostile work environment in which Black female employees were called "lazy" and "resident street walkers," according to an agency statement.[175] The settlement was the result of a lawsuit filed by the EEOC on behalf of twenty-one employees in Jackson's Denver and Nashville offices. Additionally, in November 2019, Janitorial Service Provider Diversified Maintenance Systems, LLC paid $750,000 and furnished significant equitable relief to settle a federal race discrimination, harassment, and retaliation lawsuit.[176] The complaint alleged that since January 2012, the company engaged

---

[173] "U.S. Equal Employment Opportunity Commission Public Portal," U.S. Equal Employment Opportunity Commission, accessed October 14, 2023, https://publicportal.eeoc.gov/Portal/Login.aspx.

[174] "How to File a Charge of Employment Discrimination," U.S. Equal Employment Opportunity Commission, accessed October 14, 2023, https://www.eeoc.gov/how-file-charge-employment-discrimination.

[175] Michael A. Tucker, "How to Ensure Pay Equity for People of Color," *HR Magazine*, Society for Human Resource Management, March 11, 2021, https://www.shrm.org/hr-today/news/hr-magazine/spring2021/pages/pay-equity-for-people-of-color.aspx.

[176] "Significant EEOC Race/Color Cases (Covering Private and Federal Sectors)," U.S. Equal Employment Opportunity Commission, accessed October 3, 2023, https://www.eeoc.gov/initiatives/e-race/significant-eeoc-racecolor-casescovering-private-and-federal-sectors.

in an ongoing pattern or practice of race discrimination against African American job applicants in Maryland, Washington DC and Philadelphia metropolitan areas by refusing to hire Black applicants for custodian, lead custodian, or porter positions and racially harassing a Black janitorial supervisor in the presence of customers and employees. The lawsuit also alleged that when he complained, the company demoted the Black supervisor, changed his work assignments, hours, and conditions, and then fired him. Another EEOC win came about in January 2020, and it was for Jacksonville Plumbers and Pipefitters Joint Apprenticeship and Training Trust (JPPJATT). This trust sponsored an apprenticeship program that trained participants to work in the plumbing and pipefitting industries in Northern Florida, revised its selection process, paid $207,500, and provided other significant equitable relief to settle the EEOC's class race discrimination lawsuit which sought relief for applicants who allegedly were denied apprenticeship positions because they were Black.[177] As a group of believers, utilizing your voices to file formal complaints is an act of justice not just for many today but also for the many tomorrow.

6. *Start and support Black community businesses.* Consider communal Black entrepreneurship as was emphasized in African American history. For example, in 1850, the American League of Colored Laborers (ALCL) was said to be one of the first Black American labor unions, since Black workers at this time were not allowed to join White labor unions.[178] The ALCL sought to help Black craftsmen sharpen their skills

---

[177] "Significant EEOC Race/Color Cases."
[178] Emma Fridy, "A Short History on Black Labor Movements in America," *Louisville Political Review*, February 10, 2023, https://loupolitical.org/2023/02/10/a-short-history-of-black-labor-movements-in-america/.

in agricultural and industrial industries as well as encourage African Americans to pursue entrepreneurship.

Additionally, while you are meeting with your networks and support groups, discuss business ownership opportunities as a way to combat institutionalized racism. In 2020, only 3 percent of U.S. businesses were Black or African American owned, while White Americans accounted for 86 percent of U.S. businesses.[179] Study the market or industry you seek to enter and prayerfully consider communal business ownership. Money talks. "Buying Black" helps move Black Americans toward equity and equality in this country.

Summary

In summary, racial discrimination within the workplace for African Americans is still prevalent after Title VII was passed more than fifty years ago. Yet we as believers are called to bear in mind Gospel Haymanot and the African American collective historical fight to combat these injustices within the workplace. We as believers should take into account our Christian witness, socioeconomics, and physiological and psychological factors in our fight against workplace racial discrimination. We should appreciate and remember historically that there is power and victory in a multitude when we unite to contest this type of discrimination. May we progress together to experience biblical justice in the workplace.

---

[179] Rebecca Leppert, "A Look at Black-Owned Businesses in the U.S.," Pew Research Center, February 16, 2024, https://www.pewresearch.org/short-reads/2023/02/21/a-look-at-black-owned-businesses-in-the-u-s/.

Resurrection Hope: A Future Where Black Lives Matter, Kelly Brown Douglas, Maryknoll, NY: Orbis Books, 2021. 978-1626984455. 224 pp., $26.00 (paper).

In *Resurrection Hope*, Rev. Dr. Kelly Brown Douglas shares her deep passions, sufferings, experiences, and insights as a Black individual in a society that often privileges whiteness and is antagonistic towards Black people. This book is not strictly theological or sociological; it is a culmination of Douglas's extensive experiences as a Black theologian, professor, mother, daughter, clergy member, and citizen of America. She delves into the theological conflict of understanding that while God promises deliverance, Black people continue to face oppression. The burning question is, when will God deliver?

This book is about hope, not doubt. While it may not offer explicit theological interpretations or a direct interrogation of white supremacy, it carries a profound theological energy that propels it toward the goal of *Resurrection Hope*. The book is divided into two parts: The first part, "A Corrupted Moral Imaginary," explores the existing issues. In contrast, the second part, "From Crucifying Death to Resurrection Hope," provides Douglas's wisdom and insights on addressing and repairing these problems. When considering the book's structure and title, you can think of Part One as dealing with crucifixion and Part Two as focusing on resurrection.

Part One: A Corrupted Moral Imaginary

This section opens with a recounting of the unjust killings of Black individuals during the 2020 Black Lives Matter protests. Douglas shows that the U.S. has a deep-rooted problem that requires a solution. She defends her doubts about God's ostensible lack of deliverance for

Black people by highlighting that their oppression is still very much a part of the U.S. Through this section, she offers a well-researched and nuanced interpretation of the history and current state of white supremacy and privilege that has and continues to shape the moral imagination of the U.S.

At this stage, Douglas explicates the roots of anti-Blackness, which is more than just white privilege. In a short amount of space, she details how the origins of anti-Blackness are rooted in the project of Western society itself, from Greek philosophy to the early days of the patristic, medieval, and (post-) Reformation Christianity eras. This chapter's strength is that she outlines the contours of anti-Blackness in the history of Western philosophy and theology and through the fabric of America's political and historical landscape.

In the next section, Douglas highlights various instances, events, and symbols in America's history driven by racist motives. What troubles her is not these events themselves but the underlying way of thinking—the epistemology of whiteness—that corrupts America's moral imagination. Douglas explains how an anti-Black culture can normalize its biases, shaping the kind of society America has become. She points out that "white social-cultural epistemological privilege is itself a construct that sustains a system of domination and thus undermines the possibility for a just democracy" (p. 92). This shows that Douglas is not anti-America; she's against racism. Her critique aims to help America achieve its goal of truly being a land of justice for all.

In the final part of this opening section, Douglas explores what Martin Luther King, Jr. called the great stumbling block for Black Americans' journey toward freedom: the white moderate. Here, she contrasts the intentions and teachings of white Christians with their lack of action against the daily toils of anti-Blackness. Her goal is to show that the silence from these "good Christians" results in complicity and complacency in the face of white supremacy and anti-Black policies and actions. Theologically, white Christians have, whether intentionally or unintentionally, come to view Christianity through a white lens. Douglas argues that the paradox of the Cross can help white Christians break free from America's corrupted moral imagination. This paradox can lead to love and peace, especially towards Black Americans' suffering due to white Christians' silence. She draws a connection between the Cross of Christ and the suffering of Black Americans, similar to James Cone's *The Cross and the Lynching Tree*, but distinct in Douglas's approach. Douglas's discussion of this paradox serves as a transition into the book's second half, *Resurrection Hope*.

Part Two: From Crucifying Death to Resurrection Hope

This section is filled with hope. Hope for a future where the U.S. can overcome its racist history and truly become a nation that lives up to its claim of being the land of justice for all. While the first section was descriptive, this part is constructive. It is not systematic but practical, offering real-world recommendations to move the country away from its sinful past towards a redeemed future that eradicates white supremacy and anti-Blackness. Douglas focuses on two main themes around resurrection: reparations and testimony.

By the term "resurrection reparations," Douglas is not merely joining the discussion on reparations for descendants of slaves. The terms resurrection and crucifixion here are not to be confused with Jesus Christ's Crucifixion and Resurrection. Instead, they're used analogously to describe the experiences of many Black Americans. Crucifixion represents the current suffering and solidarity with Jesus that the oppressed feel. But crucifixion is not the end; Jesus was resurrected. Similarly, the suffering of Black Americans does not have to be the end of America's story. Resurrection brings hope for a better future.

Douglas's "resurrection reparations" concept taps into God's eschatological plan for the world. Unlike traditional reparations, which focus on rectifying past injustices, resurrection reparations look toward future potentials. Douglas explains that these reparations aim to transform America's moral consciousness, providing a framework beyond monetary restitution. Instead, reparations are seen as a commitment to healing the future for the Black community and the broader American project. This framework involves acknowledging America's past through the perspective of the marginalized Black community, using the Incarnation and the remembrance of Jesus's sacrifice as mechanisms for retelling history. By drawing this connection, Douglas establishes a theological basis for truth-telling about history that honors God. Ultimately, "resurrection reparations" include a social dimension promoting healing Black individuals and communities. Douglas articulates the necessity of reparations impacting the embodied existence of Black Americans, and this must take place through active participation in justice by faith communities.

In discussing "resurrecting reparations," Douglas extends this concept to "resurrecting testimony." She acknowledges that in the past, based on her experience, she dealt with Black suffering by interpreting it through the lens of Jesus's death on the Cross, as if Black suffering was salvific for America. Douglas explains, "Essentially, the cross shows God's uncompromising solidarity with the Black oppressed even as it reflects the depth of Black oppression" (p. 186). Like James Cone, she now views the Cross as a symbol of solidarity with the marginalized, specifically Black Americans. This vision of the Cross bolstered and sustained Douglas's faith. For her, the Cross represents not an end but a departure from suffering toward a new life and reality—a new reality embodying God's justice. Therefore, the invitation is to collaborate with God to create a just future for Black people. Douglas understands the global protests for Black Lives Matter as evidence of God's Spirit at work, moving history toward God's ultimate goal of justice and safety for Black people worldwide. She concludes this second half, as well as her book, with a message of hope: that God's future for Black people will be founded not on the framework of white supremacy but on the caring love of God.

In summary, Douglas's book is a worthwhile read when approached as a spiritual journey, devotional, or testimonial that brings hope to those Black people who are experiencing suffering and those observing the suffering of Black folk in America. The book does not introduce anything particularly innovative regarding the dual issues of white supremacy and anti-Blackness in America. However, even the opening section that rehearses this dualism is valuable for readers unaware of these problems or the origins of anti-Blackness. My only critique is that Douglas did not engage much with Scripture nor construct her solution through theological *loci*. Nevertheless, this is a minor issue since it is not the book's primary focus. The book's purpose is to accompany the reader from despair to hope, from the Crucifixion to the future Resurrection: the evils committed by men during the Crucifixion do not have the final word; the Resurrection, through God's promise to bring justice, does. And for that, Rev. Dr. Kelly Brown Douglas has rendered us just a little more hope, which we need.

Leon Harris
Los Angeles Bible Training School

Do Black Lives Matter? How Christian Scriptures Speak to Black Empowerment, edited by Lisa M. Bowens and Dennis R. Edwards, Eugene, OR: Cascade Books, 2023. ISBN: 978-1666705416, 318 pp., $36 (paper).

Do Black Lives Matter? How Christian Scriptures Speak to Black Empowerment is a collaborative project featuring several essays by African American scholars. The aim is to show that, from a biblical and theological foundation rooted in the Black Christian tradition, Black lives do matter. Furthermore, Scripture is the foundation to affirm Blackness, also known as African American religious worship, theology, and culture, and to argue the centrality of justice and as a foundation for battling the oppression of white supremacy. The book is divided into three sections: 1.) "Biblical Analysis and Expressions of Black Empowerment;" 2.) "Theological Reflections and Expressions of Black Empowerment," and; 3.) "Sermons on Blackness."

Section one, "Biblical Analysis and Expressions of Black Empowerment," is a collection of seven essays that are written by scholars in biblical studies. The first two essays in this section provide the historical and theological background, while the following five essays focus on specific passages or genres. Lisa Bowens ("Hearing Scripture as Protest and Resistance") summarizes how three African American leaders—Lemuel Haynes, Richard Allen, and Fannie Lou Hamer—employed Scripture in their contexts, employing a "protest and resistance hermeneutics" (p. 3). Joseph Scrivner ("A Hermeneutics of Text and History") describes race and poverty focusing on key civil rights leaders after the March on Washington. He describes a hermeneutical lens that displays God's concern for injustice and summarizes the history of African American oppression and the accomplishments of the Civil Rights Movement. Angela N. Parker ("The Empire Will Fail:

Paul's Vision for the Church Then and Now in Romans 8") argues "that solidarity into one body means that the church then and now must purposely unite in solidarity with those who undergo high levels of imperial suffering even when that includes creation whom interpreters rarely place with the language of the 'family of God'" (p. 44). Jennifer Kaalund ("The Stories Our Bodies Tell: Black Bodies That Matter, Black Lives That Matter"), argues that for Black lives to matter, the Black body itself matters. In U.S. history, white supremacy goes hand in hand with violence against the Black body. She appeals to the symbol of the body discussed in various ways in the Letter to the Hebrews. Jaime L. Waters ("Prophet Tenacity") presents a survey of Scriptures from the prophetic books, and she describes lessons for Black empowerment today. She details the economic injustices as outlined in the prophetic books. She points out that Huldah's prophecies are pivotal in Josiah's reforms that remove false idols, which she argues is analogous to the removal of Confederate symbols of white supremacy. Dennis R. Edwards ("Protesting Police Brutality and Criminal Injustice with Paul and Silas") focuses on the African American hermeneutic that focuses on God's holistic mission of liberation. He analyzes Acts 16:12–40 to show the injustices Paul experienced by the Roman Empire, and his assertion of his rights as a Roman citizen. These provide lessons to the current context about unjust policing and identifying and denouncing injustice. Finally, Jamal-Dominique Hopkins ("Biblical Accounts of Racial Profiling and the Social Death of Black Lives") compares racial profiling by King Herod (Matt. 2:16–18) with racial profiling by the police in the U.S. He also relates this act of profiling and violence to social death, which, along with the violence and vulnerability, results in dishonor to one's very being.

Section two, "Theological Reflections and Expressions of Black Empowerment" is a collection of seven essays that are written by scholars in theology, practical theology, ethics, and history. Danjuma Gibson ("Black Lives Moved by the Bible: Moving from the Love of Power to the Power of Love") contends that preaching and teaching is an act of power. The use of Scripture to reprimand Black and Brown people in the drug abuse and HIV/AIDS crises is a religious abuse of power. When the homiletical authority is shared between the preacher and the audience, this allows a reading of Scripture that integrates our human experience, resulting in liberation and renewal. Valerie Ranee Landfair ("Hagar's Lament: Affirming Black Lives Matter through Resilience, Interconnectedness, Spirituality, and Expectancy") focuses on Hagar's plight as an enslaved and sexually assaulted woman, parallel to enslaved and oppressed African American women. Pneumatological orientation is the spirit-empowered groaning (through speaking in tongues) employed in the Bible to cope with the effects of racism. A Womanist reading of Scripture displays a resilient resistance to racism, the interconnected nature of Hagar (oppressed) with the Israelites in the Body of Christ, holistic freedom given by the Spirit that affirms Black lives, and an expectancy that the Spirit enables liberation and hope. Antonia Michelle Daymond ("Toward a Theology of Revolutionary Protest") first discusses the rise of European colonial Christianity that produces conquest, empire, and white supremacy. She contends that the ethos of the Protestant Reformation should lead to a critical examination of Protestantism, leading to the centering of the voices and experiences of the marginalized and decentering the voices that promote white normativity. Brian Bantum ("Black Bodies, Art, and Community") discusses the importance of Black art for the Black community and dignity, focusing on the role of Christian icons, colonization, and white Jesus. Through art, Black artists, oppose white supremacy. Reggie Williams ("White Supremacy Is a Script We're Given at Birth") points out that white supremacy is the paradigm of U.S. society. After arguing for a precise definition of white supremacy, he illustrates how this paradigm is a script that U.S. culture possesses. To make progress, we must recognize and remove the script of white supremacy. Y. Joy Harris-Smith ("Communicating Culture: The Beauty of Black Speech") argues that Black speech reinforces community and "reminds us of our interdependence and the need for one another" (p.

178). Culture is transmitted through communication and language. She cites several examples of the importance of Black speech. For example, Jesse Jackson's speech "I Am Somebody" proclaims the value of Black lives in the face of Black death. Vince Bantu ("'I Am Black and Beautiful': A Biblical Haymanot [Theology] of Blackness") argues that Black people are in Scripture, so Christianity and racial justice are not only compatible but are interconnected. Examples of Black presence in Scripture include the "Ethiopian" eunuch of Acts, the people of Kush as the presence of Black people in Scripture. Revelation includes Black people among all tribes, tongues, and nations. Marcia Clarke ("Migration, Adaptability, and the Utilization of Media: Black Pentecostalism Goes Global") presents the Church of Pentecost (COP), based in Ghana, as a global presence of Black Pentecostalism. After surveying a brief history of the denomination, she explains how their denomination grew through the members' migration to other countries in search of economic stability, their adaptability by expanding from the Twi language to English through the partnership with the Pentecostal International Worship Center, and the integration of modern and social media. Antipas L. Harris ("Black Protest Theology: Considering Bourdieu's *Habitus* Theory with a Comparative Analysis of Protest Approaches in the Civil Rights Movement and the Hip-Hop Generation") argues that the protest approaches in the Civil Rights Era and the Hip Hop Generation follow Bourdieu's *Habitus* Theory. This theory features three elements: "(1) the conviction that God favors the oppressed; (2) the search for refuge, elevation, and freedom in community; and (3) the need for physical engagement in freedom demonstrations" (p. 218).

The last section presents four sermons on Blackness. Luke A. Powery ("Jesus and the Borders [Luke 14:7–14]") preaches that the people at the margins matter. Jesus instructed people to sit in a lowly place so that they could be exalted. Sitting with sinners and tax collectors could be analogous to sitting with Black people. Just as the lives of the marginalized matter in that time, so Black lives that are marginalized matter today. Efrem Smith ("Rise of the Liberating Church") presents the biblical foundation for God as one who cares about Black bodies. There is a need for holistic liberation—from the cosmic sin caused by the demonic powers, the sin that affects each individual, and the sin that brings about unjust structures and enables racism, etc. His focus is Moses, the one who brings liberation and points to the ultimate liberator, Jesus Christ. Donyelle McCray ("Feast Day for Saint Harriet") argues for the inclusion of African Americans from the past in our liturgies in the Black Church. Her point is that churches should honor the ancestors, which highlights the African American witnesses (referring to Heb. 11:1–16)—showing African Americans who "embody Christian virtues" (p. 250) into our liturgies. She examines Harriet Tubman's life and story as an example. David D. Daniels III ("A Decriminalizing Gospel and Empowering Maneuvers") discusses the importance of the courts and criminalizing. In his examination of James's letter, he argues that the rich are the ones who prosecute and have people arrested. They can use the court system to criminalize the poor and marginalized. He calls for justice, envisioning James's letter as an act of protest. The message is to love neighbors and enact justice through decriminalizing the systems and structures that promote white supremacy and racism.

The book contains short essays, most of which are ten to twelve pages. Each essay includes discussion questions and a bibliography of works cited. Each essay is compelling, whetting the appetite for more discussion. It contains a variety of hermeneutical approaches so that one can see the spectrum of thought among African American biblical scholars, theologians, ethicists, historians, and preachers. The depth of research represented in each bibliography, in this writer's opinion, is worth the price of the book. This book is highly recommended as a collection of African American scholarship addressing the critical issues of the value of Black lives, Black liberation, the priority of justice, and the dismantling of white supremacy in our theology and cultural practices.

Kenneth Reid
Tabernacle Community Church

Africa and Byzantium, Andrea Myers Achi, New Haven, CT: Yale University Press, 2023. 978-1588397713. 352 pp., $65.00 (cloth).

Andrea Myers Achi provides an impressive work of inviting interdisciplinary scholars to showcase Africa's renowned economic, religious, and cultural art from late antiquity to the early modern period. Africa's position in the arts has been understudied due to the negative portrayal of Africa and the dominant position the Roman Empire has given itself. This catalog highlights specific African regions and gives them their artistic props where they are long overdue. The book has three major sections: "From Carthage to Aksum: Africa in Late Antiquity," "Bright as the Sun: Africa After Byzantium," and "Legacies: Black Byzantium." I will highlight distinguished entries from each section.

"From Carthage to Aksum: Africa in Late Antiquity." This section recounts North Africa's strong Christian faith by examining Christian monasticism in Egypt. One can find distinct artistry in monasteries with influential figures (such as St. Shenoute) and animals painted in vivid color on ceilings and walls. Visual art is also represented in mosaic floors, baptismals with a jeweled cross, and ornaments that transports one's sight of it into a heavenly place (p. 34). North Africa became a notable center of learning and literature, birthing the Christian theology we know today due to African church fathers like Tertullian of Carthage, Augustine of Hippo, Athanasius of Alexandria, and Cyril of Alexandria. Art at this time included paintings of the saints and biblical Apostles to indicate how the Christian culture held them in high regard. Sixth century Egyptian pieces such as the *Icon with the Virgin Enthroned* woven tapestry speak to this reverence (p. 45). Visual art can also be seen in earthenware like flasks of Saint Menas that were transported from

Rome to Egypt and were said to hold miracles that were recorded in Coptic, Greek, and Ethiopian documents (p. 55). Mosaics were prominent during the fourth through sixth centuries, and they most likely depicted social, civic, and religious life and displayed the pride of the wealthy (p. 76). Likewise, mosaics included Jewish symbols (menorahs) in places like Tunisia in the remains of a synagogue, which speak to the presence of ancient Jewish communities in Africa (pp. 81–84). Moving to Nubia, they developed a relationship with Rome via Egypt, as Egypt had an existing trade relationship in the First and Second Cataracts of the Nile River. Between the third century BCE and the early centuries CE, Egypt shared Roman influences with Nubia and vice versa (p. 86). Nubian influence can be seen in Byzantium with beakers notched with elephants. One can also find Roman influences of vine-leaf wreaths on pottery in Meroitic jars (p. 87). Meroitic influence in the early Byzantine world is discernible in Rome's pottery, iron and wood art that visualize cultural and political relationships (pp. 89–92). Ethiopia is highlighted in this period, focusing on its relationship with Byzantium. Axum interacted with Greek culture to the degree that some citizens knew the Greek language. King Ezana's conversion to Christianity around 340 CE can be found in his understanding of the Christian Trinity in an Axumite inscription in Greek (p. 104). One can find basilicas and pendants that mimic cross motifs that were representations found in both Axum and Byzantium (p. 105). Axum was on mission to spread Christianity in Nubia and Arabia. Some of their influences concerning traditions, narratives, and visual motifs were influenced by the Greco-Roman and Jewish Mediterranean world (p. 106). Axum's early conversion in the fourth century was fortified in the truth of Scripture as they ignored the Roman religious doctrine of Arianism. They held fast to the fully human and fully divine nature of Jesus Christ, and this is reflected artistically (p. 107). Also emphasized in this section is the "Representations of Black People in Mediterranean Antiquity" which is shown through art like the *Bust of an*

African Child portraying a difference of race in art. The African child is depicted with wider or different features (e.g., nose, texture of hair) than could be found around Samanud, Egypt (p. 114).

In "Bright as the Sun: Africa After Byzantium," Vince L. Bantu commences this section detailing the seventh-century Islamic invasion that sparked migration and trade in other nearby regions (pp. 127–128). Muslim travelers documented many of their routes in seeking new territory for commerce and trade. Zavilah was a major port along the North African coast where slaves were forced to migrate to the Sahel. Additionally, since Islam was introduced, it battled against indigenous religions as well as a predominant existing Christian population in North Africa. Christianity was so firmly rooted that, according to Egyptian Christian historical texts, Alexandria's Patriarch was the head of Christians in Kairouan, Tripoli, Egypt, Ethiopia, and Nubia during the tenth century (p. 128). Coptic book production in the ninth century (primarily used for Egyptian monasteries) began to grow even after the Islamic conquest in Egypt (p. 143). The painted triptych with crucifixion, likely from Egypt in the thirteenth to fifteenth century, depicted events that came before Christ's crucifixion. Egyptian monasteries contained folia from five different languages (Ge'ez, Syriac, Coptic, Arabic, and Armenian) that compare New Testament Acts and Epistles between the twelfth and fourteenth centuries (p. 157). These visual pieces speak to the enduring Christian community in Egypt. Artistic influences were also drawn from African Pilgrimages to Sinai, since Sinai was a monastic center and influential for many Africans due to its centrality in the biblical text. Despite Muslim forces trying to conquer Nubia, they could not due to the Christian Nubian army. One can find a painting depicting Nubian archers that speak to the skill they had in defeating the Muslims (p. 129). Nubia's visual Christian culture could be seen through hundreds of churches and monasteries, along with multilingual books that were traded to northeast Africa (p. 147). While Egypt came under Islamic rule, Nubia continued as an independent Christian empire up until the sixteenth century; before this period Nubia adhered to the Coptic Church (p. 130). Nubia's empire increased as the imperial power of Byzantium started to decrease. Nubia embraced their own language as they labeled themselves Dotawo as they took pride in who they were (p. 178). Nubia became an intersection between Egypt and Ethiopia for trans-Saharan trade routes. Sahelian kingdoms such as Mansa Musa's Mali Empire in the fourteenth century were a major gold export to various parts of Africa and other world regions. Although Mansa Musa adopted Islam, there were Christians that existed in the Mali Empire that maintained the gold, hence, Christianity spread to West Africa. Trading of goods introduced trading of languages, religion, and culture among African regions. The Axumite Christian Kingdom remained unbothered by rising Islamic powers; representation is shown from Ethiopian artists such as Fre Seyon that accentuate distinct Ethiopian iconography depicting biblical characters such as Abraham, and Paul and Peter (pp. 131, 257).

Lastly, in "Legacies: Black Byzantium," Kristen Windmuller-Luna moves us further into the medieval period by showing the unmovable faith of Ethiopia as she inserts a quote from Emperor Zarʻa Yaʻqob from the 1450s *Book of Light* about his kingdom's strong Christian beliefs. Regarding Ethiopia's relationship with Byzantium during this time, art representations can be found in similar church architecture in both Ethiopia and Byzantium (such as arches or chancel screens), yet local distinctions are highlighted per their individualized cultures (p. 208). Differences in Ethiopia and Byzantium's Christian beliefs are brought forth at this time, such as Byzantium's fourteenth-century mournful art piece of Jesus dying on the cross versus an Ethiopian art piece shining the light on the cross being empty, highlighting the salvation of Jesus to the world (p. 212). This part of the book reminds us of how Byzantium has been given more attention concerning its artistic, religious, and cultural achievements rather than Ethiopia, which has outlived Byzantium for many centuries. This also demonstrates how scholarship should continue to highlight this unequal narrative and spotlight Ethiopia's Christian artistic achievements (p. 213). In the fourteenth century, Ethiopia created many intense pigmented panel paintings such as the Virgin Mary or other saints, designed as a sign of Ethiopia's reverence and admiration for such persons (p. 240). The cover of this book includes half of a fifteenth to sixteenth-century diptych displaying the iconography of Saint George slaying the dragon to save the princess of Beirut (p. 252). At the end of this book, Andrea Myers Achi encourages her readers to progress towards "A Critical Geography" as she emphasizes that this book's objective was to educate on Africa's rich, independently distributed artistic innovations. Readers should embrace a new narrative about Africa's art contributions and look to the past to inform our future. *Africa and Byzantium* displays the beauty of embracing infused art from different continents and cultures. This catalog was a breath of fresh air to read as Western academia has praised the Roman Empire's contributions to Africa. This literature provided a greater appreciation of the cultural achievements of Africa not only to Byzantium but to the world.

Charonda Woods-Boone
Meachum School of Haymanot
NAIITS: An Indigenous Learning Community

www.ingramcontent.com/pod-product-compliance
Lightning Source LLC
Chambersburg PA
CBHW030557080526
44585CB00012B/400